THE DIARY OF WILLIAM FISHER OF BARROW 1811 to 1859

edited by

William Rollinson

and

Brett Harrison

Centre for North-West Regional Studies
University of Lancaster
Occasional Paper No. 15
1986

General Editor: Oliver M. Westall

Cover: Barrow Harbour from the east, showing the method of loading ore in 1844 (from a water-colour drawing by Mrs Michaelson). Courtesy of Furness Museum.

ISSN 0308-4310
ISBN 0-901-272-191

This volume is the fifteenth in a series of occasional papers in which contributions to the study of the North-West are published by the Centre for North-West Regional Studies in the University of Lancaster and are available from there. The general editor will be pleased to consider manuscripts of between 10,000 and 25,000 words on topics in the natural or social sciences and humanities which relate to the counties of Lancashire or Cumbria.

PREVIOUS TITLES

Windermere in the Nineteenth Century
Working Class Barrow and Lancaster 1890 to 1930
Handloom Weavers' Cottages in Central Lancashire
Flowering Plants and Ferns of Cumbria
Early Lancaster Friends
Traditional Houses of the Fylde
Peter Newby: 18th-Century Recusant Poet
North-West Theses and Dissertations 1950–1978: A Bibliography
Lancaster: The Evolution of its Townscape to 1800
Richard Marsden and the Preston Chartists, 1837–1848
The Grand Theatre, Lancaster: Two Centuries of Entertainment
Popular Leisure and the Music Hall in Nineteenth-Century Bolton
The Industrial Archaeology of the Lune Valley
Roman North-West England

Grateful acknowledgement is made of financial assistance from the Kirby Archives Trust in support of this publication.

Printed by Mather Bros (Printers) Ltd Preston

CONTENTS

PREFACE

Barrow was one of the most striking boom towns of mid-Victorian England. Geography and technology combined to enable steel and shipbuilding to draw migrants from all over the British Isles to create an entirely new, thriving industrial community. Before this, the area had been a largely agricultural economy, only modestly influenced by outside affairs through a small port and difficult overland travel. Small farmers passed lives marked by the regularity of the seasons, disturbed only by the immediate realities of crops, weather, accident, illness, birth, death and marriage. Industrialisation took Barrow into a wider world in which local events were no longer almost entirely explained by circumstances in Furness.

William Fisher farmed land round the site now occupied by Barrow Town Hall on the eve of these changes. His Journal reflects those local rural preoccupations and illustrates life in Furness before its transformation. But he was well placed to notice the beginnings of change. During his life he saw its foundations laid as the port of Barrow expanded, the Furness Railway was constructed, mining developed and a community gradually took shape. This edition of his Journal, helpfully amplified by the editors' introduction and supporting explanatory notes, will therefore provide an important source for all interested in the emergence of modern Barrow.

Oliver M. Westall

Introduction

The Diary and Its Author

William Fisher was a Low Furness yeoman farmer, one of that group of independent 'statesman' so admired by William Wordsworth. He was born in Barrow in 1775 and died in 1861; Margaret, his wife, and a member of the Cock family of Kendal, was born in 1784 and died in 1866. Throughout his long and active life, William Fisher kept a diary of local happenings in Low Furness and in the village of Barrow in particular—the births, marriages and deaths, the seed-time and the harvest, the catastrophes and the commonplace. Although his spelling and grammar are erratic, his diary is no less valuable for that, for he chronicles the day-to-day life of a small agricultural hamlet on the shores of Barrow Channel during the most dynamic period of its history. Within the 48 years covered by the diary the small farming community of Barrow grew into a young and vigorous industrial town founded on the wealth of the rich, red haematite iron ore of Furness and the slate of the Kirkby area.

Fisher provides a fascinating glimpse of Barrow during its transformation from a small agricultural hamlet into a brash nineteenth-century town, but at the same time he records the passing of the yeomanry of Low Furness. William Fisher stemmed from a long line of yeoman farmers, but by the time of his death in 1861 the numbers of these 'statesmen' had declined considerably; the late Professor G. P. Jones calculated that in 1829 in the Parish of Dalton, which included Barrow, the yeomen amounted to 23.4 per cent of the farmers whereas in 1849 the figure in the same parish had declined to 13 per cent.[1] There are few eye-witness accounts of Barrow's early agricultural and industrial history and this makes the Fisher manuscript all the more important, but it is more than merely an interesting piece of local history—it has a much wider significance for it may be considered to be one of the human documents of Britain's industrial revolution.

The diary forms only part of the Fisher manuscript; the remainder consists of detailed farm accounts and household transactions from 1810 to 1828. Unfortunately, lack of space prevents the publication of these accounts here, but information from them has been incorporated in this introduction.

The Fisher manuscript is privately owned, but thanks to the generosity of Mr Russell Rowlandson of Ulverston and to the Cumbria Record Office, Barrow, where it is now housed on permanent loan, the diary can be published in full for the first time.

The Village of Barrow

In common with many other Low Furness villages, Barrow was founded as a grange or home farm by the Cistercian monks of Furness Abbey. First mentioned in monastic records in 1190, it seems that the grange of 'Barrai' was situated close to the site occupied by William Fisher's farmhouse in the nineteenth century.[2] Barrow remained essentially a small farming hamlet until the nineteenth century: indeed, in 1780 the village consisted of five farm houses clustered on the shore of Barrow Channel about four miles from Dalton, the nearest town.[3] By 1801 the number of dwellings had increased to eleven and the population was estimated to be approximately 65: four years later Dr William Close, a medical practitioner and local author, was able to write of:

> . . . the hamlet of Barrow, a small sea port situated about three miles to the south-west of Furness Abbey, is . . . a place to which invalids often repair to bathe in the summer season.

It contains two commodious Inns, and is the first sea port in Furness for the exportation of iron ore, oats, malt and barley.[4]

By 1822 the number of houses had increased to twenty, and a blacksmith, butcher and shoe-maker were resident in the hamlet. Although iron ore was exported from Barrow in 1745, it was not until 1782 that it was shipped in any quantity; in that year the Newland Iron Company, based near Ulverston, constructed a quay to facilitate loading operations and eight years later a wooden pier was built, enabling larger vessels to be loaded. The foresight of the Newland Company sparked off a period of growth; in 1833 a second pier was constructed, followed in 1839 and 1842 by two more—the potential of Barrow had been recognised and a new seaport had been born.[5] In 1846 the Furness Railway connected the iron ore mines near Dalton and the great slate quarry at Kirkby with Barrow, in 1852 the first Barrow ship was launched and in 1859 the iron furnaces were lit for the first time; Barrow had become a 'boom-town', the 'English Chicago', and it is against this background that the Fisher diary is set. However, the diary is essentially a log-book of a yeoman farmer, recording the main events in the farming year together with comments on the weather, the cost of hired labour, and the price of grain. From such data it is possible to piece together a picture of the economic geography of Low Furness in the early nineteenth century.

Furness Agriculture in the late eighteenth and early nineteenth centuries

Furness agricultural development undoubtedly suffered from the isolation of the area; in 1772 when farmers in East Anglia and the Midlands were rapidly improving agricultural techniques, Thomas Pennant, referring to this remote area claimed that

> . . . the inhabitants of these parts have but recently applied themselves to husbandry. Among the manures, sea-sand and live mussels are frequently used; but till within these twenty years the use of dung was scarcely known to them[6]

Pennant noted, however, that one of the main crops at this time was beans, which were exported to Liverpool 'for the food of the poor enslaved negroes in the Guinea trade'. Thomas West, writing in 1774 was equally unenthusiastic about the state of Furness agriculture; he complained that

> One general obstacle to improvement and the advancement of agriculture in Furness is the mixed lands or township fields . . . [7]

Moreover, W. B. Kendall, the nineteenth-century Furness antiquary and naturalist, claimed that until the mid-eighteenth century the land was 'neither drained, cleared, or manured'.[8]

By the late eighteenth century new agricultural methods were being introduced: writing in 1795 the agrarian writer J. Holt classed Low Furness with the Fylde and the lower Lune Valley as the three main wheat-producing areas of Lancashire[9] and by the first decade of the nineteenth century Dr William Close was able to argue that Walney Island was

> . . . as productive of wheat, oats, and barley as to deserve the appellation of the Granary of Furness.[10]

The first indication of the 'improvement movement' was the enclosure of the open fields; most of the township fields were enclosed at the end of the eighteenth century, but in several cases an exact date cannot be given because the fields were enclosed by private agreement and not by Act of Parliament. However, by 1810 Close noted that Low Furness was 'divided into large enclosures by verdant hedges'.[11] One of the first Low Furness villages to enclose its common fields was Hawcoat; by 1731 most of the fields had been divided. Salthouse followed in 1734, then Cocken in 1741, Newbarns, 1750 and Biggar and North Scale on Walney Island by 1778. Sadly there is no record of the enclosure of the Barrow township fields although the field name 'reins' is evidence of their existence.[12]

By the time William Fisher commenced his diary in 1811 the pattern of mixed farming which characterized Furness agriculture in the nineteenth century had been established; R. W. Dickson, writing in 1815, records that Low Furness was suited to most varieties of arable crops, 'but wheat, barley, oats and a few of the pulse kinds are at present principally raised'.[13] Although a few farms such as Gleaston Castle farm and Holebeck farm exceeded 200 acres, most Low Furness farms were small. An analysis of the Tithe Commutation Schedule for Dalton-in-Furness (1842) shows that William Fisher's farm consisted of slightly more than 85 acres, and a similar study of the Cragg holdings at Biggar on Walney Island indicates that this farm was approximately 58 acres at the same time.[14]

Unfortunately, the Fisher diary does not catalogue the major improvements in agricultural practice, but W. B. Kendall's assiduous study of the neighbouring township of Salthouse enables certain deductions to be made.[15] Wheat cultivation was stimulated by the high prices during the American War at the end of the eighteenth century and was further encouraged by the Napoleonic Wars; oats also grew well and Kendall suggests that some fields grew this crop perpetually. Oats, together with smaller amounts of wheat, barley and malt, entered into the export trade of Low Furness. Potatoes were not widely grown at Salthouse, but William Fisher records planting them in 1821 (4th June), and turnips were sown broadcast until about 1815 when they were abandoned, to be re-introduced again as a field crop about 1840, although Cragg continued to grow turnips at Biggar until 1817.[16] Clover was grown on Walney Island, and probably elsewhere, in 1808, and vetches in 1813, while about the same time grass seeds were being improved by experimental means, while in Barrow in 1817 'Early Poland corn' and 'Winchester ryegrass' were planted. In the early nineteenth century, seaweed or 'tangle' was used as a manure, and guano was first introduced in 1850. Sub-soil drainage which had transformed the farming pattern in parts of south Lancashire was introduced into Low Furness about 1842.

Entries in Fisher's diary clearly indicate that his farm at Barrow was organized as a mixed farm; wheat, barley and oats were sown, a hay crop was taken from the meadow in July, and seed grass was mown in June. Potatoes were a common crop after 1821, beans and peas were grown, and in 1818 a crop of clover was mown. Dairy cattle were kept and the Fisher accounts show that butter and cheese were an important item in the farm economy. Close links with a fell farm, Fenwick on the slopes of Black Combe (Grid Ref: 168894) appear to have been forged; visits to the farm at sheep clipping time are mentioned on several occasions and members of the Bowes family from Fenwick often visited the Fisher household in Barrow. In August 1854 Fisher records that Thomas Bowes brought eleven sheep to Barrow from Fenwick and this might explain the link between the two farms; traditionally, fell farmers have brought their yearling sheep to Low Furness for wintering, but in this case August seems a little early to bring sheep for wintering.

During the early part of the nineteenth century the Napoleonic Wars, and later the Corn Laws kept the price of wheat high and encouraged its growth but the consequent high price of food resulted in considerable hardship for the Furness peasantry. Another contemporary local diarist, William Fleming of The Rowe, Pennington near Ulverston, recorded in his diary[17] in 1812 that the price of oats was 22 shillings a bushel, barley 31 shillings a bushel, and wheat 72 shillings a load, and comments vividly on the general unrest among the working classes. William Fisher does not mention this dissatisfaction but his accounts record that in 1812, he was selling wheat at 85 shillings a load and barley at 26 shillings a bushel. Table A gives the prices of wheat sold in Barrow, compiled from the Fisher accounts; clearly, during the period 1810–1828 the price of wheat was highest between 1810 and 1813. Although wheat continued to be grown in Barrow, it never again achieved this high price range. A series of wet summers in the 1830s resulted in a succession of poor harvests and in 1834 Fisher complained that

> . . . wheat this year is afaling Crop particularly in the Island of Walney and money other places it was quite washed of in Winter and obliged to be sown with Oats in the spring and from the wetness of the Weather of late Wheat will be sadly sprouted . . . [18]

TABLE A

Approximate price of wheat per load at Barrow

Year	Price Range per Load						
	£	s.	d.		£	s.	d.
1810	2	8	0	to	3	12	0
1811	2	12	6	to	2	15	0
1812	3	9	0	to	4	5	0
1813	2	4	0	to	3	10	0
1814	1	18	0	to	2	15	0
1815	1	13	0	to	2	17	0
1816	2	10	0				
1817	1	14	0	to	2	7	6
1818	1	19	0	to	2	12	0
1819	1	10	0	to	2	0	0
1820	1	5	0	to	2	6	0
1821	1	5	0	to	1	18	0
1822	1	3	6	to	2	2	0
1823	1	5	0	to	2	2	0
1824	1	16	0	to	2	7	0
1825	1	17	0	to	2	6	0
1826	1	19	0	to	2	1	6
1827	1	12	0	to	2	2	0
1828	1	14	0	to	2	6	0

One of the most valuable aspects of the Fisher diary is his careful recording from 1811 to 1856 of the dates when he began to cut his grain and the dates when the harvest terminated. Using this information it is possible to construct a graph (Figure 1) from which certain generalizations may be made. On the whole, it appears that the grain harvest occurred between the first week in August and the last week in September. However, in High Furness the harvest was generally later, a reflection, partly, of the greater rainfall and the higher incidence of cloud cover. This discrepancy between the harvests resulted in the migration of itinerant reapers from Low Furness to High Furness as the crops ripened and the harvest progressed, but in 1834 Fisher lamented

> . . . Shearers 4/– and 3/6 per day owing to so maney being wanted the Harvest commenced in all parts of the Country at the same time . . . [19]

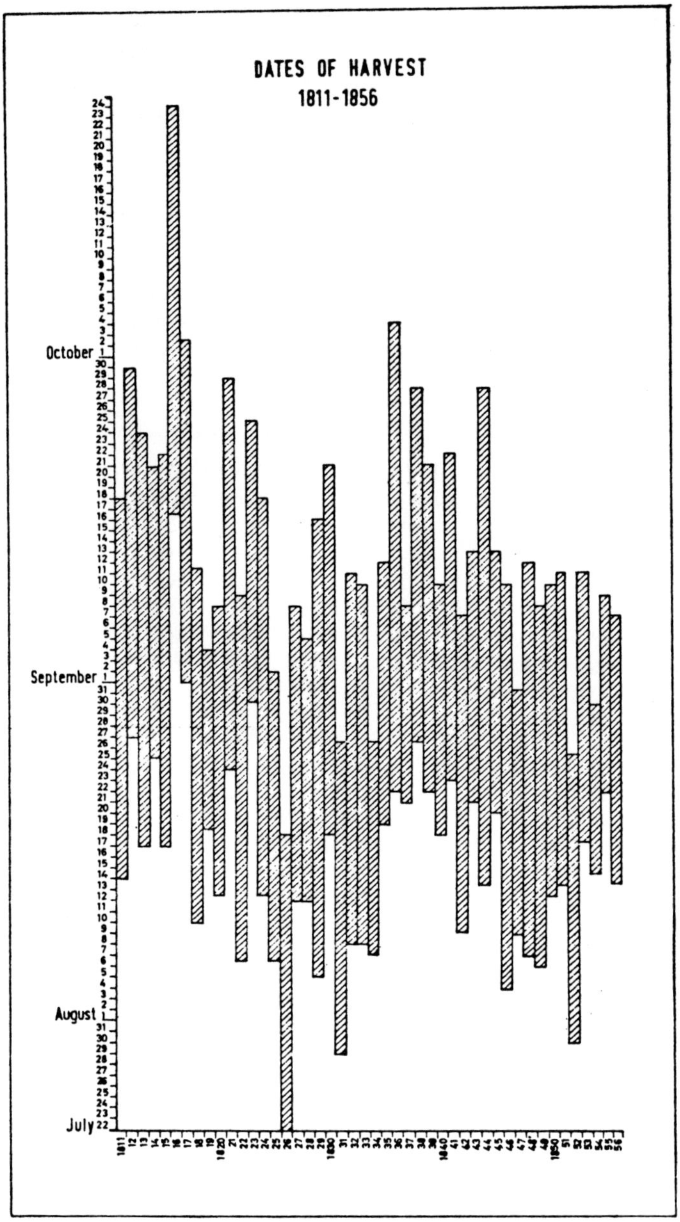

Fig. 1

A closer examination of Figure 1 reveals certain anomalies, for example, the extremely late harvest of 1816, the early harvest of 1826, and the generally late harvests of the early Victorian period. Assuming that any extra hands remained more or less the same, and that the amount of grain to be harvested remained fairly constant, an explanation might be sought in past climatic records. In November 1816 William Fleming commented on the inclement summer of that year:

Friday, 8 November, 1816
It is a circumstance remarkable and to be remembered and handed down to Posterity that owing to unseasonable and Winterlike Summer this Harvest has been later than has ever been remembered: there is at this Time much Grain particularly Oats out in the Fields. It is very uncommon to see Fields of Grain some uncut and some standing in the shock or stook, covered with snow and frozen together, but it is the Case this Year[20]

And these dismal events were emphasized by William Fisher three days later when he recorded on 11th November 1816

. . . a snow fell in the morning near a foot thick there was also some Barly out and 60 or 70 stouks of Wheat out at Denderon which was Compleatly covered with snow there was also some Beans to Shear & a deal unhoused . . . .

These reports have been confirmed by the work of the late Professor Gordon Manley who used early climatological observations to compile a table of monthly mean temperatures for the Lancashire plain between 1753 and 1945.[21] From this it can be seen that the mean summer temperatures in 1816 are significantly lower than in preceding or succeeding years:

	J.	F.	M.	A.	M.	J.	Jul.	A.	S.	O.	N.	D.
1814	25.6	34.6	37.5	48.7	47.5	53.2	59.5	57.4	54.7	45.4	39.9	38.1
1815	32.5	42.9	43.6	45.4	53.4	56.6	58.1	58.1	55.1	50.1	37.4	35.0
1816	36.6	36.1	38.4	43.3	49.2	54.1	55.3	56.9	52.1	49.8	38.8	36.8
1817	39.8	42.6	41.2	47.0	47.2	57.7	56.3	55.4	54.9	42.6	47.6	35.1
1818	38.9	36.6	38.6	42.6	52.4	60.1	63.1	57.8	54.8	53.2	48.5	38.9

Professor Manley suggested that the disastrous summer of 1816 probably owed its origin to a series of violent volcanic eruptions in the East Indies;[22] such explosions cause a high-level dust screen which may reduce incoming solar radiation, particularly in the summer months. Certainly the abysmal summer of 1816 was not confined to Cumbria; in Dumfriesshire the cutting of barley, usually the first grain to ripen, did not begin until 20 September.[23]

The harvest of 1826 was early (Figure 1) and this was possibly a response to higher mean temperatures in June, July and August.

	J.	F.	M.	A.	M.	J.	Jul.	A.	S.	O.	N.	D.
1824	40.0	40.3	40.0	45.3	51.2	56.2	60.0	58.2	55.7	47.7	42.8	39.5
1825	37.7	38.5	40.9	47.1	52.5	56.5	61.8	60.6	58.6	50.8	40.2	39.7
1826	32.0	42.9	43.1	47.0	52.7	62.9	63.1	62.1	56.0	51.0	39.2	41.7
1827	35.1	33.6	41.7	47.7	53.1	57.3	60.8	57.8	56.1	52.8	43.5	43.6
1828	40.3	40.7	43.4	46.0	53.6	58.9	59.7	59.4	57.0	49.5	44.7	45.0

Unfortunately no rainfall figures for Low Furness exist for this period, but in Kendal during this year only 43.5 inches of rain fell and 42 years later 1826 was still spoken of as 'the dry summer'.[24]

The lateness of the harvest between 1835 and 1841 follows a pattern which was repeated throughout much of Great Britain; the consequent poor harvests brought hardship to thousands. Even after the repeal of the Corn Laws in 1846, the price of grain and foodstuffs remained high. Fisher recorded that in April 1847,

. . . Potatoes Sold in Ulverstone Market at 2/2 p. stone and Eggs at 2d per Egg.

There appears to have been no sudden decline in the amount of arable land in Furness after 1847 and, indeed, Garnett in 1849 was able to claim that

> . . . Furness seems to be the redeeming feature in Lancashire farming. In the soil, the class of farmers, and their general management this district would not suffer comparison with other more favourable and accessible parts of England.[25]

After 1850 improvements in communications with the rest of Lancashire further encouraged Lancashire agriculture. J. D. Marshall[26] has pointed out that the establishment of a regular steamship service from Roa and Barrow to Fleetwood enabled the produce of Furness farms to reach the industrial markets of Preston and south Lancashire. After 1857, when the Ulverston–Lancaster line was completed, the same produce could be transported by rail.

The Fisher diary provides certain other information concerning the weather of north Lancashire during the early decades of the nineteenth century. For example it seems that 1831 was a favourable year, and certainly the harvest was early (Figure 1); Fisher records that 'the Greatest part of the Grain was secured by the end of August . . . ', and adds that the seed-time was 'a dry season'. A similar fine seed-time occurred in 1852 when Fisher wrote: '. . . a very fine season never knew the ground work better', and on 19th July 1825 he recorded

> . . . had got all our Meddow hay the 2 or 3 suckeding days was the hottest I ever remembered we got 72 car Lods of hay.

1845 was another good year for both seed-time and harvest, and during the harvest period from 20th August to 13th September only one quarter of a day was lost because of poor weather. During March 1852 an unusually dry period occurred and on 30th March Fisher wrote that 'the land in verry good order we had a verry little rain from the Latter end of Feby till this time . . . ', and on 1st April '. . . Considered to sow our potato and Turnip land with Oats Instead of Barley the weather being so fine . . . '.

As well as his regular observations on farming weather, William Fisher also recorded the more unusual meteorological phenomena such as the early snow on Black Combe in south Cumberland on 7th October 1829 and the very late snowfall which occurred on 9th May 1837. In 1833, storms created havoc with shipping in the area; on 11th June 1833 several vessels were blown from their moorings and sunk, and on 31st December there occurred

> . . . a heavy Gale of Wind which drove the schooner Iris of Whthaven from the moorings and through the high end of the Old Quay till within 10 feet of Josephs Fisher Gardin wall the same vessel with two others was drove on shore behind the Ile of Walney about five Weeks before in a simmler Gale, one of them an Irish Brig and the other a Duch Galliot the wear all three partly loden with salt and all got of again but most part of the salt was lost.

An equally fierce storm blew up in January 1839 when houses were unroofed, haystacks destroyed, and 'there was a great loss among the Shipping and many lives lost . . . '. The storm which had the most far-reaching effects occurred on 27th December 1852; Fisher records this as '. . . a perfect Hurricane doing great damage all over the Country'. During this storm the embankment connecting Roa Island with the mainland was extensively damaged and the island and the embankment were subsequently sold by the owner, John Abel Smith, to the Furness Railway Company.[27]

Reports of shipwrecks, particularly on the exposed western shores of Walney Island, are common in the diary (Table B); all manner of ships seem to have foundered on this coast, from Manx vessels (18th June 1833; 5th February 1835) to a Portuguese brigantine carrying wool (20th December 1839). Timber salvaged from these wrecks seems to have been auctioned, for Fisher records in his accounts the purchase of such wood; officially, this timber belonged to the Duke of Buccleuch as Lord of the Manor of Furness.

TABLE B

Shipwrecks on the Furness Coast recorded in William Fisher's diary

Date	Name and type of ship	Port of Origin	Cargo
31st Jan. 1825	Sloop 'Aurora' 30 tons	Preston	—
6th Nov. 1825	Brig 'Susanna'	Whitehaven	in ballast
27th Mar. 1827	'Commerce' 70 tons	Ulverston	Gunpowder
1st June 1829	Sloop 'Vennox' (refloated 3rd June)	Cardigan	iron ore (?)
11th June 1833	Not specified	—	salt
18th June 1833	Fishing boat	Isle of Man	—
23rd Nov. 1833	Brig	Ireland	salt
	Galliot	Holland (?)	salt (?)
31st Dec. 1833	Schooner 'Iris'	Whitehaven	—
5th Feb. 1835	Smack	Isle of Man	wheat
7th Jan. 1839	4 or 5 vessels driven ashore on Foulney Is.	—	—
20th Jan. 1839	Brig	Whitehaven	300 tons of coal
20th Dec. 1839	Brigantine 'Tejo'	Lisbon	wool
31st July 1843	'Fanny'	Fleetwood	slates
9th Feb. 1848	Smack 'Friends'	Newquay	corn

Although not connected with meteorological conditions, one of the most intriguing of the diary entries deserves mention—the earthquake of 1835. On 20th August, Fisher wrote: 'a shock of an Earthquake was felt here and for 20 Mile distant' but he does not indicate the severity of the shock, however, the *Annual Register* for 1835[28] records that the earthquake was felt as far south as Liverpool and was felt with 'considerable violence' at Ulverston, Kendal, Garstang, Preston and Blackburn.[29]

Industrial Development in the early Nineteenth Century

Just as the Fisher diary illuminates development of the agricultural landscape of Low Furness, so, too, it contributes to the knowledge of the development of the industrial landscape. In the early decades of the nineteenth century the industrial wealth of Furness was largely derived from iron ore and slate. Before the construction of the piers at Barrow between 1790 and 1842, iron ore had been shipped from loading-points around the Furness coast, but these diminished in importance with the development of the hamlet as an ore shipment centre. However, until the 1840s the production of iron ore from Furness Mines was not great; H. W. Schneider suggested that before this date the output of the entire district did not exceed 30,000 tons.[30] The most productive mines during this period were the Whitriggs and Lindal Moor pits, and ore was transported from the pit-head to Barrow in crude carts. By 1841, exploitation had moved south-westward and ore from Thwaite Flat was being transported to Barrow; Fisher recorded on 1st February that year '. . . the Harbour Master entered up his situation at Barrow also same Day the Wet [Thwaite] Flat Iron Ore was first led to Barrow.'

Fig. 2 Barrow Island and Barrow Channel *circa* 1835. The boats are almost certainly carrying iron ore from Barrow Village. From an oil painting by Mrs Michaelson.

Conditions in the iron ore mines during the early decades of the century were primitive and fatalities were common. Ore was raised by means of a horse gin, and pit drainage was almost non-existent; mining ceased when the water table was reached, and miners were raised and lowered in buckets. The entries in Fisher's diary serve to emphasize the appalling conditions in the Furness mines. On 25th November 1828 two men were

> . . . sufacated by the foul air at Crosgates Iron Ore pit there was two others in at the same time which escaped with dificulty by accinding the Shaft in the bucket . . .

Similarly, on 26th May 1838, two men were suffocated in a bizarre accident at Stainton pit when a cabin at the pit-head caught fire and the smoke descended into the shaft. Subsidence and roof-falls were depressingly common; in March 1840 two men were killed by subsidence at Lindal mines,

> . . . the were dug out immediately but quite dead several others wear upon the Same place but all escaped unhurt . . .

One of the miners killed was over 70-years-old. In the following year a miner was killed at Butsbeck mines '. . . by aporishon of the roof comming down upon him tow or three more had a narrow escap . . . ', and in February 1854 'five men blocked up in a Iron Ore Pit at Park near Dalton by the bursting in of a pond of Water three was drowned and two taken out alive but one died the fowling day'.

In spite of primitive methods the output of Furness ore increased from 30,000 tons in 1841 to 300,000 tons in 1851;[31] in this year the great Park ore body was discovered, and a few years earlier, in 1846, the Furness Railway had cemented the link between the iron mines near Dalton and the slate quarries near Kirkby, with the shipping piers at Barrow. By 1859 heavy industry had been established on the shores of Barrow Channel—one of the last entries written by Fisher records the opening of the Barrow Iron Works:

> The Iron Furnaces was opened at Hindpool Barrow Witnessed by several gentlemen who came by special Train on the 18th October owners Messrs Hannah and Schneider. It was a Galla and a beautiful day for the season.

Thirteen years earlier Fisher had recorded the opening of the Furness Railway, perhaps without realising the significance of the event . . .

> Railway on the 30th April [1846] the locomotive engin belonging to the Furness Railway was for the first time driven up to Kirkby Ireleth. After staying for some time She departed for Barrow[32]

and on 24th August

> the Railway from Roa to Dalton was opened for passenger.

In 1852 the first ship to be built at Barrow was launched, a forerunner of a long line of merchant and naval vessels. On 15th September, Fisher recorded that

> The first New Ship Built at Barrow 180 tons was Launched the day was beautiful all the Vessels had their Flags hoisted. She was Christened by Mrs. Roper Snr the Jane Roper in respect to Mrs Thos Roper of Newland House.[33]

These three events, then, the opening of the Furness Railway, the launching of the first ship, and the firing of the Hindpool iron furnaces, are important landmarks in the industrialization of Barrow and the Furness area, events which remained significant long after William Fisher's death.

Communications

As well as describing the opening of the Furness Railway, the diary also illuminates other aspects of the communication network in Furness. Until the extension of the Furness Railway in the 1850s, Furness was isolated by the Cumbrian mountains, the Duddon estuary, and Morecambe Bay.[34] The turnpike road around the Kent and Leven estuaries, completed in 1820, was an improvement, but the journey to or from Lancaster took many hours, consequently the more direct cross-sands route from Ulverston to Lancaster at low water was much frequented; indeed a regular cross-sands passenger service commenced running in 1781 and remained in operation until the Ulverston–Carnforth–Lancaster line was completed in 1857. In addition to the saving of time, the journey across the sands was sometimes more pleasant than a journey along the turnpike as William Fleming noted in his diary in 1809:[35]

> The sands were perfectly good but the land roads unpleasant on Account of the Dust which was raised by carriages and Carts upon the Roads.

However, the tides and quicksands claimed many lives during crossings of the sands and Fisher records several such deaths. In January 1841 two young men were drowned on Leven Sands 'and when found next morning the horse and gig was stuck fast in the channel and one of the men entangled aboute the step of the gig the other was found a little below in some fishing nets the wear a long way below the foard'. Similarly, in 1846, nine people attempting to cross the sands from Ulverston to Cartmel were drowned, 'the wear all in one Cart every one with the horse Perrished it was suposed that the weare the wors for licquor'. Other fatalities on the sands are reported in February 1817, January 1837, and November 1848. Although Barrow had a postal service from 1847,[36] no details are given in the diary but the opening of a telegraph system in 1854 is casually reported on 25th July that year. It seems that a robbery had been committed in a Barrow inn and the thief had stolen

> . . . a pocket Book containing Notes and gold to the amount of £50 also a purse containing 20 sovereigns the Telegraph was only finished that morning to transmit the message to Ulverstone He was taken at the Abbey [Furness Abbey] stood his trial at Lanc^{r} [Lancaster] on the 7 Augt and sent to be imprisoned in the House of Correction 12 months.

The Social Scene

The diary throws some light on the contemporary social scene in Low Furness. Within this isolated farming community, William Fisher was obviously a man of some importance; he attended church regularly and, in February 1816, the accounts show that he paid £19 for a seat in Dalton church. On 26th May 1817 he '. . . attended a metting of the sides men as one, for the first time'. His religious conviction was clearly strong for he and several elderly people received Communion in the Fisher home in January 1853 and again in January 1858, and he notes with interest the opening of a new chapel in 1844 to serve the needs of Barrow, Newbarns, Hawcoat and Salthouse villages.[37] Although there was no Roman Catholic church in Barrow village in the early part of the nineteenth century, some members of the community clearly belonged to the Catholic faith for Fisher mentions in 1836 the death of a child '. . . aged about 6 Months Interd at Walney without any serimony being of the Romen perswason'.

In any small, rural community, rumour and gossip abound—and Barrow was no exception. Fisher was not averse to recording the scandals of his day; on July 1st 1834 John Stephenson married Isabella Brockbank and Fisher comments '. . . she was brot to bed 26 Octr folling'. In 1842 he records the marriage of Nathan Dickinson to Catharine Hodgson '. . . the bridegroom aged 19 and the bride not Quite 14 years', and in 1824 Thomas Park was accused of rape by a servant girl but was acquitted by a jury at Lancaster assizes. In 1817 Fisher laconically records 'the Revd John Trowton Married to Betty Layland after being a disconslate awiddower 15 weeks'.

Perhaps one of the most striking features of the diary is the catalogue of deaths; indeed, it could be argued that Fisher had a morbid curiosity about sudden death and violent fatalities. Lugubrious though this undoubtedly is, it is none the less valuable for it throws light on fatalities in the local iron mines, on deaths by burning, on suicides and on drownings on the sands of Morecambe Bay. Almost certainly, Fisher derived his information from local gossip but there is also the possibility that he acquired some of his facts from the pages of newspapers such as the Ulverston Advertiser and the Lancaster Gazette.

William and Margaret Fisher had four sons and two daughters (Table C), all of whom received some kind of formal education. Mary, Margaret, Richard and William James attended Captain Barrow's school in the village,[38] and Margaret later attended a boarding school in Ulverston. Even in this small agricultural village, social graces and learning were not entirely neglected—Richard and William James were given dancing lessons, and in 1825 Fisher paid £1. 4s. 0d. for a copy of Edward Baines' *History of Lancashire*. In June 1825 the Fisher household received for the first time a copy of 'the Newsepaper Called the Sunday times'. Entertainments were few; occasionally a dance would be held in the village (2nd August 1811), but more often in the Assembly Rooms at Dalton or Ulverston. Visitors were regularly received at the Fisher farmhouse, and in turn William and his family paid visits to friends in the neighbourhood; the regular visits to Fenwick farm in south Cumberland for the sheep shearing were almost certainly social occasions. Cock-fighting was a most popular Furness sport, and the accounts show that William Fisher sometimes visited the mains; Cumberland and Westmorland wrestling was another form of entertainment which was well attended. In October 1851 Fisher reported 'the great rusling mach at Ulverston Jackson and Atkinson suposed to be 7,000 Spectators present'—in fact this was an underestimation for it is believed that over 10,000 people saw Atkinson of Westmorland defeat Jackson of Cumberland by three falls to one.[39]

TABLE C

The Fisher Genealogy

William Fisher b. 1775 d.1861	= Margaret Cock of Kendal b. 8 January 1784 d. 1866

Margaret b. 1809 d. 1856	= Matthew = Denney	Mary b. 1811 d. 1852	= Jas. Bolton	Richard b. 1814 d. 1890	= Eliz. Denney	Wm. James b. 1816 d. 1882	= Eliz. Battersby m. 1842	John b. 1820	Henry b. 1828 m. 1858

Sources: 1. 'Some Furness Pedigrees'—ms. by J. P. Smith, Lancashire Record Office.
2. William Fisher's Diary.

The Barrow community had no resident medical practitioner until the second half of the century; following the death of Dr William Close in Dalton in 1813, Dr Allen seems to have attended to the needs of the villagers but many minor ailments were treated with ancient remedies some of which Fisher records in his diary. In March 1830 Fisher mentions a death from smallpox in Dalton, but this outbreak does not seem to have caused undue concern, possibly because Dr Close had introduced vaccination against the disease in 1799.[40] However, four years later in 1834, an outbreak of cholera resulted in considerable alarm:

> Oct. Elizabeth the wife of Nickler Fisher of Little Mill Stile began in the Cholera on the night of the 7 and died on the 8 her Grand Daugher residing with her begun on the 12 and dies on the 13th, Nicholas Fisher husband of the above Elizabeth Fisher begun on the 14 and died on the 15 a Daughter took it a few days after but recovered again it threw the Countrey in to such an alarm it was thought nessary to prevent its farther spreading to burn every article in the House the Clock alone was saved and it had the desired effect. I write this Decr 22 and there has not been another Case the loss will be mad up by the Parish.

In the absence of a resident medical practitioner, it is not surprising to find that William Fisher records a number of remedies and cures ranging from preparations to relieve scalds and burns to cures for rheumatism, toothache and blistered feet. In addition he records such useful household hints as how to kill flies without poison, how to remove bed bugs, and how to mend broken china. Some of these he copied from various newspapers but it seems likely that he also recorded some of the traditional potions and cures of the Low Furness area, passed down from one generation to the next.

Of the six children of William and Margaret Fisher, the two girls died in early middle age. Margaret (born 1809) married Matthew Denney of Dalton and died on 7th July 1856 aged 47. Mary (born 1811) married James Bolton, an innkeeper of Ulverston, and died on 12th December 1852 aged 41. Richard the eldest son was born in 1814 and died in 1890, and William James was born in 1816 and died in Barrow in 1882. John was born in 1820 and in May 1842 found employment with Mr Carter, a Liverpool druggist. In August 1844 John sailed from Liverpool to New York, and then travelled to Brownsville, Pennsylvania[41] to the home of his Uncle, William Cock. After an absence of twelve years he revisited Barrow (16th December 1856) but returned to the United States in 1857 (2nd April 1857); he was to visit Barrow once more, in 1869, but by this time his parents were dead. Henry, the youngest son, was born in 1828, and became a partner in the firm of Messrs Fisher and Coulthard, drapers, of King Street, Whitehaven. William Fisher's last entry in the diary is dated 21st November 1859; he died in 1861, aged 85, his wife Margaret died five years later, aged 82. In 1874 their son Richard sold the farm to Barrow-in-Furness Corporation and the building was demolished.[42] Within a few years the Fisher estate was lost beneath a rash of red-brick expansion.

Footnotes to Introduction

1. Jones, G. P. The decline of the Yeomanry in the Lake Counties, CW_2 LX11. 219.
2. Barnes, F. *Barrow and District*. 1951, 93.
3. Barrow Channel was enclosed in 1867 to form the Devonshire and Buccleuch Docks. The Devonshire Dock is currently the site of the Trident Submarine Shed of British Shipbuilders.
4. Close, W. in West's *Antiquities of Furness*, 1805 edition, 384.
5. Before the construction of the piers at Barrow, ships in ballast were floated onto the shore at high water at various points around the Furness coast, the ballast was then unloaded and iron was loaded on board from crude carts before the next high tide lifted off the ships once more.
6. Pennant, T., *A Tour in Scotland and a Voyage to the Hebrides* (1772), printed in William Mavor's *The British Tourists Pocket Companion*, i, (1809). Pennant makes the mistaken assumption that agriculture in Furness had always been backward; in the monastic period the granges of Furness Abbey had produced quantities of wheat, oats, barley and other produce, and the dung or 'worthings' from the abbey stables had been used as a manure.
7. West, T., *Antiquities of Furness*, 1774, 23.
8. Kendall, W. B., Salthouse, Barrow Naturalists' Field Club Transactions, vi, New Series, 33.
9. Holt, J., *The Agriculture of Lancashire*, 1795, 57.
10. Close, William, An Itinerary of Furness and the Environs, Transcript by T. A. Beck, Manchester Central Reference Library.
11. Close, W., *loc. cit.*
12. Rollinson, W., unpublished M. A. thesis 'The Rural Landscape of Low Furness', Manchester University, 1961.
13. Dickson, R. W., *A General View of the Farming of Lancashire*, 1815, 232.
14. Rollinson, W., *op. cit.*

15. W. B. Kendall, like William Fisher, came from a long line of Low Furness farmers. During the second half of the nineteenth century and early twentieth century, he kept detailed notes based on the records and folk memory of his father and grandfather, together with his own observations on local history and geology. These form the basis of the Kendall collection now housed in the Cumbria Record Office in Barrow.
16. Cumbria Record Office, Barrow, Furness Collection, Z278.
17. Manuscript diary of William Fleming, microfilm, Barrow Public Library and Lancaster University. Extracts published in *The Countryman*, vol. LV, 1958.
18. Fisher's spelling and punctuation have been retained in the extracts and in the transcript.
19. On 17th August 1806 William Fleming of Pennington recorded '. . . this day being the first of the season, great numbers of Irish came over to reap, who caused the prices to be lower than usual'.
20. Fleming, William, manuscript diary, *op cit.*
21. Manley, G., Temperature Trend in Lancashire, 1753–1945, Quarterly Journal of the Royal Meteorological Society, vol. 72, No 311, 1946.
22. Manley, G., *Climate and the British Scene*, 1962, 301–2. Manley argued that the cold summers of 1784, possibly 1845, 1860, 1884, 1902 and 1912 may have been products of similar volcanic eruptions.
23. Wood, J. D., The Complicity of Climate in the 1816 Depression in Dumfriesshire, Scottish Geographical Magazine, April, 1965, 8.
24. Webster, C., On the Farming of Westmorland, Journal of the Royal Agricultural Society, 2nd series, vol. 4, 1867, 12.
25. Garnett, W. J., Prize Report on the Farming of Lancashire, Journal of the Royal Agricultural Society of England, vol. 10, 1849, 35.
26. Marshall, J. D. *Furness and the Industrial Revolution*, 1958, 245.
27. Melville, J. and Hobbs, J. L., Early Railway History in Furness, Cumberland and Westmorland Antiquarian and Archaeological Society, Tract Series LX111, 1951, 32. The cost of repairing the embankment following the storm was £1,042. 8s. 2d. During the same storm Walney Island was breached to such an extent that *The Ulverston Advertiser* newspaper claimed that it would have been possible to sail a boat from one side of the island to the other.
28. *Annual Register*, 1835, 128.
29. A similar earthquake was reported at Rampside and Barrow on 15th February 1865. See Bolton, J., *Geological Fragments*, 1869, 253–9.
30. Schneider, H, W., On the Haematite Iron Mines of Low Furness, Cumberland and Westmorland Association for the Advancement of Science, No. 10, 1884–5, 106.
31. Schneider, H. W., *loc. cit.*
32. This was not Fisher's first reference to the Furness Railway; that occurred on 17th May 1845 when he notes a coroner's inquest on 'a work man on the rail way'.
33. The *Jane Roper* was registered as a vessel of 94 tons.
34. When the Furness Railway was opened in 1846 it had no connection with any other network, consequently the rolling stock and the locomotives had to be brought to Barrow by sea from Fleetwood.
35. Fleming, William, *op. cit.*, 23rd June 1809.
36. Melville, J., and Hobbs, J. L., Furness Travelling and Postal Arrangements in the 18th and 19th Centuries, Transactions of the Cumberland and Westmorland Antiquarian and Archaeological Society, New Series, xlvi. On 12th April 1847 James Fisher, aged 17, was appointed Postmaster. Before this date there was a foot-post between Dalton and Barrow, which began in 1836.
37. Number 251 Abbey Road now occupies this site.
38. Captain James Barrow was a cousin of Sir John Barrow, traveller, writer, founder of the Royal Geographical Society and Secretary to the Admiralty. Captain Barrow was a pilot in Barrow Channel but around 1815 he began to teach in a school in the village. He died in Ulverston in 1859.
39. Rollinson, W., *Life and Tradition in the Lake District*, 1981, 190.
40. Gaythorpe, H., William Close, Barrow Naturalists' Field Club Annual Reports, XVII, 170.
41. Brownsville is situated on the Monongahela River some 30 miles south of Pittsburgh.
42. Gaythorpe, H., Supplementary notes on the Village of Barrow, Barrow Naturalists' Field Club Annual Reports, XVII, 188.

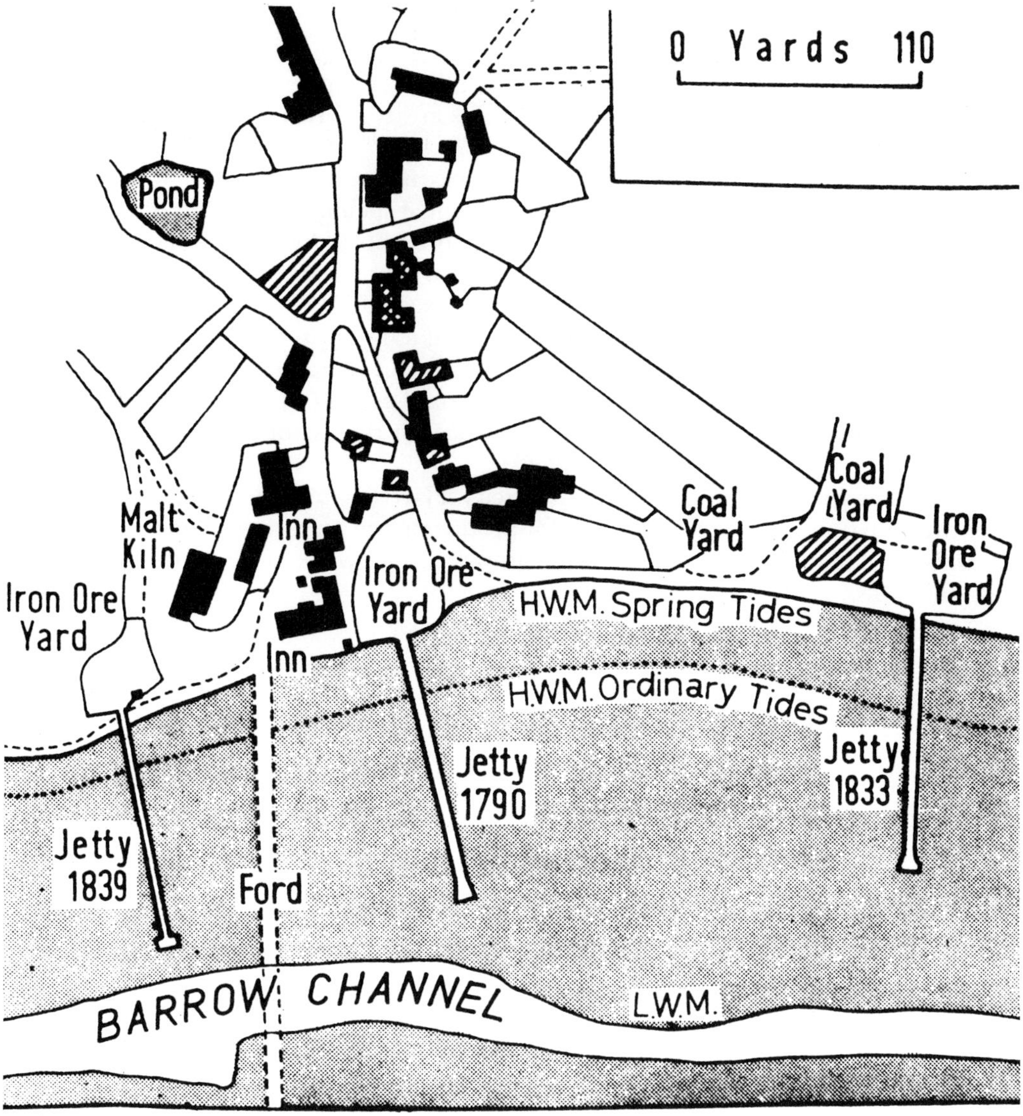

BARROW VILLAGE, 1842

(based on Tithe Map and W. B. Kendall's Ms. Survey)

 William Fisher's farmhouse

 Other property owned by William Fisher

Fig. 3

EDITORIAL NOTE

The original diary is hand-written, 20 cms × 32 cms in size, with 130 leaves and bound in vellum. Apart from the diary entries, the volume includes detailed farm accounts for the Fisher estate from 1810 to 1829, together with recipes and remedies.

The editors have adhered to William Fisher's original spelling and marked the end of a page in the manuscript with the notation ||. Square brackets indicate editorial inserts. The inconsistency in spelling is reflected in the recording of months and years. These have been simplified by the elimination of most duplicate entries.

The editors wish to thank Mr R. Rowlandson of Ulverston for allowing the Fisher manuscript to be printed, Mr Ron Smith of the Barrow Public Library for his help with the illustrations, and Mr Aidan Jones of the Cumbria Record Office, Barrow in Furness. Acknowledgement is made to HM Stationery Office for the use of the Ordnance Survey Maps.

Grateful acknowledgement is made to Felicity Harrison for checking the transcript against the original and to Marilin Pidduck for producing the typescript. The editors would like to pay special thanks to Mrs Marion McClintock for her work in seeing this publication through the press.

William Rollinson
Brett Harrison

Diary of William Fisher of Barrow

1811

Notes from the firs of March 1811

March

27 Miss Betty Busher from Kendal and Miss Elleson from Crosthwt along with 2 Miss Garnets from Dalton called in at our house and took Dinner with us
30 very pleasant and warm Weather begun to sow Corn got through on the 5 April

April

7 Hail showers and frost in the morning
13 Mary Fisher Christned Cr. Louder Jn. Coward Ann Show & Emmey Garnet stood sponcers[1]
20 B Richd Came over to see us returned on the 22nd[2]
22 Ann Show left us for Kendal She had stopd with us about a forthnight
a Cow at Sourby Hall had lingered all Winter was thought to be in a declining state so was Killed thinking that she would never mend when Opend a Hagworm or adder was found in the Inside 16 inches long
29 Joseph Fisher of Dalton Departed this life aged 78 year
30 Peggy Dixon Delivered of a son
a man killd at Kirkby slate Quarries also one at the Ioren ore Pits

June

7 Got swarm of Bees
9 Wm Bleasdal Married to George Atkinson daughter of Dalton
13 George Peethall of Black beck, Carrier between Ulverston and Kendal for Many years Departed this Life

July

21 Mrs Forste of Ulverston Departed this Life aged 73
22 James Hool of Dalton departed this Life aged 92

Augt

2 Stabls Ball at Barrow
3 Mr and Mrs and Miss Greenhow from Kendal Drunk Tea at our house
12 Mrs Hind of Kendal with Mr Rawlinson of Northend came to Drink tea at our house
July 11 John Coward married to Betty Garnett of Dalton
17 James Hunter of Titup departed this life aged 71
24 Nancy High Married to Thos Dilworth Garstang
Begun to shear Wheat 14 Augt.
Shore out 18 Sepr 1811||

Sept

22 Richd & Betty Lowder [Lowther] & there Daughter Margt came to get Dinner & spend the Day at with us

Octr

31 Thos Richardson of Old Park near Ireleth Departed this life aged 81 years

Novr

7 Wm Kendal Died by excessive drinking of rum at Ramside from a wrecked ship aged 18 years

17 my wife & I our two little Girls went to Dine & drink Tea with Richd & B Lowder [Lowther] of Roosecoat

30 Agnes Case of Manner[3] married to Thos Kendal of Stank

Decr

25 Thos Bows went from hear to home[4]

1812

Feby

1 Ellen Kirkby Married to Jon Ruke from near Cockermouth

8 Jane Fell married to Jon Rigg

29 Cr Lowder [Lowther] Married to Margt Gould of rose Cote

March

24 Wm Fell of Hindpool Departed this Life aged 63 years

May

26 Alice Chapman of Kendal Departed this Life aged 74 years

June

4 Rebeca High Departed this life aged 17 years

Augt

2 R & Betty C & Margt Lowther came to Dine and Spend the Day at our house B Richd & his Wife with A Clark & Miss Clemmonson came to Dine & Spend the Day went to Ulverston same Day Brother & Wife was on there way home from the Isle of man

4 Mrs & Miss Barrow of Newton came to Dine & Drink Tea with us

9 My Father & little Margt went to Dine & Drink Tea with Richd Lwder of Roos-Coat

23 I was at Thos Bowes and found him well
24 Emma Garnett departed this Lif aged 23 very much Lamented by all her friends & accquentance
27 begun to Shear Wheat

Septr

30 done shearing 4 oclock in afternoon

Octr

10 Betty Barrow brought to bed of a Daugher
18 Margt & I with little Margt went to Spend the Day with Richd and Betty Louther of Roos coat
25 Thomas Bows was at our house||

Nov

8 I went to Kendal returnd on the 11 Nov found all Friends well

1813

Jan

1 1813 I went to Thos Bows and returned on the 3 nst a young man of the name of Kitchin was found dead near Swincead[5] on Saturday after Xmass day 1812

Feb

9 Thos Simpson of Dalton departed this lif aged [?]

May

6 Brother Richd was here from Lancaster
15 Thos & Betty Bows came to see my father was very poorly at that time
Doctor Close Departed this Life in the 39 year of his age much and Deserved Lamented by all who knew him[6]

July

5 Betty Kirkby married to John Idle

Augst

17 began to shear

Septr

24 Shore out about 4 oclock in afternoon

Octr

3 Richd & Betty Louther came to spend the Day with us
18 a young man servant to Thos Harrison aged 26 Died by exessive Drinking

December

5 Brother Richd cane to see my Father he beeing poorly
6 Betty Fisher of Dalton Departed this life aged 72

1814

March

27 I went to See our Friends at Kendal and found all well

April

4 begun to sow Corn Done of on the 11
9 John Jackson of Leece departed this life aged 78

May

11 Done sowing Barley
8 Thos Bows came to see us & took smiler[7] with him

June

11 Thos Bows was at our house and returned on the 12
16 my Father by Law left here for Kendal after stoping with us about 13 Days
19 Thos Bows came with 2 carts of peats and took two Calvs back with him

July

14 Ann Show came from Kendal to see us
17 Philip Hartley of Dalton Departed this Life aged 64
21 James Cock of Kendal Departed this Life aged 71

Augt

14 R & B Louder came to Dine and spend the Day with us
25 begun to Shear

Septr

21 had done Shering

Octr

17 Thos & Margt Bows came to see us
20 My wife returned from Lancaster after staying about a fortnight
30 My wife & I [and] childer went to dine with Richd Louder||

1815

May

1 Saml Coward Died May 15 aged 1

July

23 Mrs Parker, Mrs Casson, Mrs Smedders & Miss Clark of Ulverston Dined and Drunk teas with us
27 Betty Burns & her 2 childer came to see us from Lancaster on the way home to Wthaven

Aug

6 Richd & Betty Louther also Chr & Margt with Jon & Ellen simpson was at our house to Dine and spend the Day with us
8 James Butcher of Cockin [Cocken] Departed this life aged [?]
17 Begun to shear

Septr

22 had done shearing

Decr

2 Mr Richd Show died aged 63

1816

March

7 a child Burned to Deth at Scales by it Close taking fire whilst the Mother was gone for water

April

1 Begun to sow Corn had done on the 11th

June

27 My Brother in Low Jon Cock Came from America to see his Friends and relations in this Country he left Barrow at the above date on his return to his family

Augst

18 Richd & Betty Louther with Chrir & Margt came to dine at our house R & Betty stud sponcers with Mr Simpson & my wife to Wm James[8]

Septr

16 begun to Shear

Octr

23 shore out

November

10 my Wife and me with the Childer went to Rooscoat to Dine & spend the Day it was then very hard frost

11 a snow fell in the morning near a foot thick there was also some Barly out and 60 or 70 stouks of Wheat out at Denderon which was Compleatly covered with snow there was also some Beans to Shear & a deal unhoused in the afternoon it came on a storm of rain & Wind & continued so During the night To Day 12 a fine Clear Day

1817

February

18 Doctor Huddelston Married to Miss Proctor of Dalton

29 A violent Storm of Thunder & Litining such as was hardly ever remembered accompanied with a gale of wind, a horse was killed at Duddon Grove belonging to Richd Towers Esq and one had its leg brock at Whinful [Whinfield] in Pennington a man of the name of Louis was Drowned the same morning in Crossing Ulverston sands owing to the Liting and storm||

28 Mrs Trowton of Walney Departed this life aged 62 years

April

1 I went to Kendal to see our Friends and found them all well and returned on the 3rd

5 begun to sow corn got Done on the 16th April a very Dry season 2 Childeren Died at our poor house by eating swedish turnips

6 Mrs Garnett of Dalton died aged 57 years

6 Betty Postlethwaite of Newbarns only Daughter of James Ray of the same place Died in Child bed much lamented aged 22 years

21 Wm Briggs of Ulverston Lowyer [Lawyer] hanged himself in an out house not fare from there & had hung a forthnight before he was found

20 Bought a Gray Stag 4 years Old of Wm Turner of Lyth for 18..18

May

20 My sister by Law & three childer from Lancester came to spend the Day with us accompanied by her Sister & Mrs Parker from Ulverston

26 I attended at a metting of the sides men as one, for the first time[9]

June

15 Laid our Cows out
20 Thos Macon of Dalton Killd by a horse Striking at him he Lived about 24 hours after in great aggany
17 the Revd John Trowton Married to Betty Layland after being a disconslate awiddower 15 weeks

July

3 a Child Killd at the poor house about 5 years Old by a horse 2 other boys making the horse gallop over it he only lived about 4 hours after
12 I went to see Thos Bows and found them all well
23 Richd Richardsons wife of Biggar Died in Child bed with only about half an hour sickness she was taken to Cumberland to be Interd

Augt

24 Rich & Betty Louder also Christopher and his Wife came to spend the Day with us
24 John Dixon[10] & his sister from Pennybridge came to take Dinner to spend the Day with us

Septr

1 Begun to shear
3 Margt returned from Kendal

Octr

3 Shore out
19 Bella High married to James York Mr. Michaelsons Groom
26 My Wife & myself with Margt Mary & Richd went to Richd Louder to Dine & spend the Day
27 Laid our Milk Cows in the house||

1815

[Apparently a later insert]

I got 2 Cart Load of Eller powls from near thwaite Mill and laid Low Stable Scaffold with a part of them and covered it with Oack slabs that I got from the Cartpenters yard I also studded and gisted the 2 rooms Over the Kitchen with apart of them and had 3 Ladders Made all this was done in 1815 this I write as a memorandum that it may be seen how such like wood may last

Wm Fisher

1829

the above is quite gone to decay will be obliged to be made anew next summer the decay equally drie as well as wet *Nov 1 1827*

1818

Jan

20 Begun to plow March 23 had done Plowing

March

17 Thos Bows Brought me 10 Bushels Oats for seed and took 10 of Mine with him back

April

2 Begun to Sow Corn Done sowing Corn on the 20 April

May

23 had done sowing Barley Sowed none before the 11
23 Laid our Milch Cowes out Beeing fine drie and warm wether

June

9 I went to Kendal to see our Friends and found them all well
24 Begun to Mow clover 29 Laid our horses out

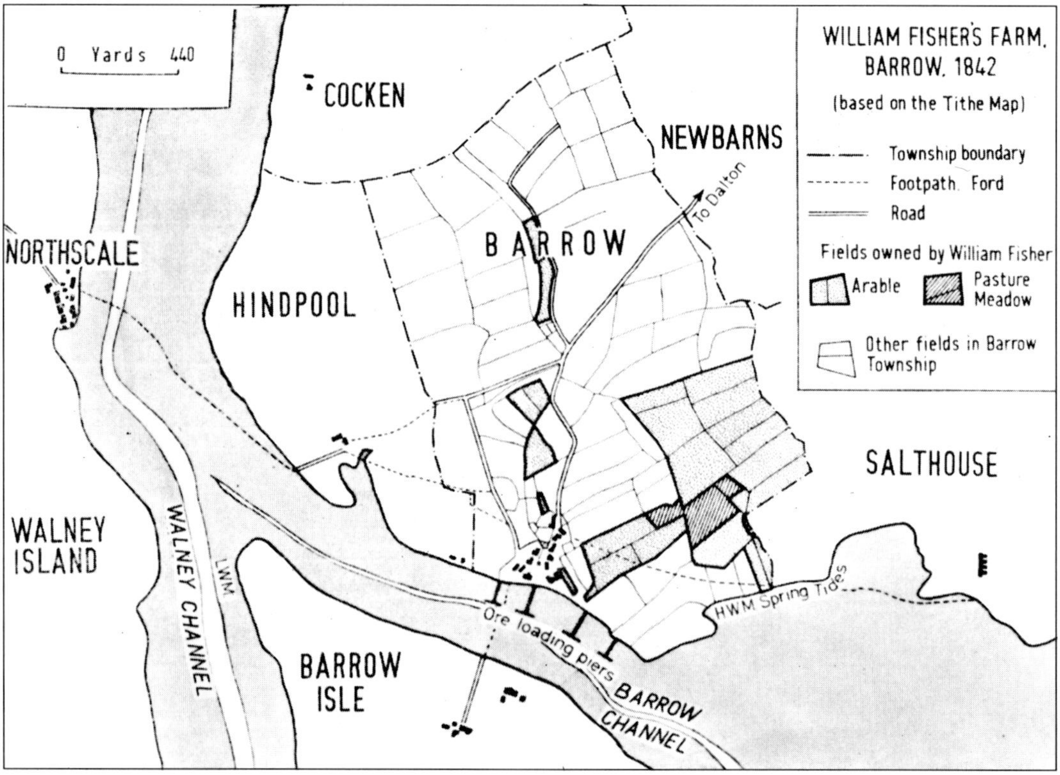

Fig. 4

July

1 Begun to Mow our Meddows 17 had got all our Meddow hay

Aug

10 Begun to Shear Septr 12 Shore out
11 Joseph Fisher Daughter Mary Died aged 7 years
16 Willm Cragg Died very suddenly aged 51 years

Octr

3 Mrs Barrow of Newton Died of a Cancer in her Brest aged 57 years
15 Laid our Cows in the House
20 Margt Simpson Died aged 84 years

Novr

26 Archibald Ferris 2 Childer Died of putrid sore throte or Inflamation on the lungs one aged 7 years and another aged 4 years the wear bothh Interdin one Grave

Decr

14 begun to plow
we had 117 Bushels Oats of the Crop of 1818 besides what the horses eat

1819

Feby

2 I went to Kendal and returned on the 4
12 Margt Thompson of Dalton Died aged 92
13 a Child was Burned to Death at Ulverston by its Close takying Fire in the absencence of its Mother it had been attempting to put apan on the fire about 6 years of Age
24 a young Man at Wholebeck [Holbeck] had his hand Chatred by the Bursting of a gun that it was obliged to be taken off a little above the rest||

March

1 Docter Allen Married to Miss Agness Gibson of the Island of Walney

April

7 Begun to sow Corn had done on the 16th

May

22 had Done sowing Barley
25 Laid some of our Milk Cows out
26 Mary Fell Died aged 68 years

June

15 Begun to mow our Seed Grass

July

6 Begun to mow our Meddows
11 Mr Heslem Exise Officer married to Robt Greendwood Daughter of Walney

Aug

18 begun to Shear Sept 4 Shore out

Sept

27 begun to sow Wheat had done on the 29

Octr

17 I went to Lancaster to the Sessions
21 Laid our Milch Cows in the house
22 Laid our 2 Mares in

Novr

7 Mr Troughton Son Died aged 2 years
13 Thos Gibson Married to Miss Hool of Ulverston

1820

Jany

1 Lenard Gould Married to Margt Lowder Both of Roose Coat
Do Wm Hunter Died aged 34 Leaving a Wife and Seven small Childer
Do Frank Clark of Stainton was Killd by a fall from a scaffeld aged [?]
26 Brother Henery Cock from Holm Lift here on his return home[11]
29 King George the III Died Aged 82 years

April

10 King George th IV Proclamd 1821 July 19 King Gorge IV Crowned
10 Begun to Sow Corn had done on the 15

May

12 had Done Sowing Barley
20 Laid some of our Milk Cows out

June

24 Laid our Horses out
24 Begun to mow our Seed Grass

24 A Salor was found on Salthous Sand which had been drowned a month before out of a boat at Peel by means of it upacting [upsetting] there was 3 more in the boat at same time but wear saved||

July

1 James Sowrey Garnett Died aged 22 years
8 begun to Mow our Meadows
8 Thos Bows Sheep Shearing
16 Miyls Gibson Wife Died in Child Bed aged 33 years
21 had got all our Medow hay

Augst

12 Begun to Shear had done on the 8 Septr

Septr

16 had done with Howsing

Octr

2 Begun to Sow Wheat had done on 4th
18 Laid our Milk Cows in
Do Laid Bonny in

1821

Jany

16 Begun to Plow had done on the 17 March

April

3 John Garnett of Ulverston Intered aged 67 years
6 Begun to Sow Corn had done on the 28
28 Mary Fell of Hindpool Died aged 40 years

May

8 begun to sow Barley had done on 19
29 Laid some of our Milk Cows out
30 Mary Falsha Died aged 71 years[12]

June

4 Set the latter end of our potatos
14 Thos Robinson of Newbarns Died aged 42 years
16 Mrs Fresh of Newbarns died aged 43 years
22 Thos Brogbank of Salthous Died aged 72 years
23 begun to Cut our Seed Grass

July

4 begun to Mow our Meddows had done on the 11
7 Thos Bows Sheep Shearing
13 had got all our Meddow hay without any Rain been very hot & dry weather

Augt

23 begun to Shear had done on the 29 Septemer

Oct

10 begun to Sow Wheat had done 11
24 Laid Bonny in
27 Laid our Milch Cows in

1822

Jany

15 begun to Plow
16 Miss Isabella Butcher married to Wm Lesh of Hollowmire

March

29 a child Burnd to Death about 3 years old by its Close taking fire at Conkle near Rampside

April

2 begun to sow Corn a had done on the 9 April||
13 Miss Bland from Lyth came to spend a few Days with us

May

13 begun to sow Barley had done on the 22 May
25 Laid some of our Milk Cows out

June

15 begun to Mow our Seed grass
24 begun to mow our Meddows had done on the 6 July
had got all our Medow hay on 17 July

July

27 Laid our two Mars [Mares] out

Augt

6 Begun to Shear had done on the 9 Sepr
20 Had all our Wheat Housed 30 had all our Oats Housed

Septr

16 had all our Barley housed
19 Chr Wilkinson Died aged 84 years[13]
26 begun to Sow Wheat had done on the 8 Octr

Octr

16 John Crag Died aged 83 years
16 Captan Barrow Daughter Jane Died aged 7 years
23 Laid our Cows in house

Novr

13 Laid Bonny in

Dec

31 Jane Kendal Died aged 63

1823

Jany

16 John Nixon of Biggar in Walney Died aged 89
25 Mrs Bolton of Old Park Died aged 52
25 Mathew Hunter of Dalton Interd aged 63 years

Feby

16 Begun to plow had done on the 8 April

April

8 Begun to sow Oats had done on the 16
21 Joshue Towrs of Dalton Died Aged 89
23 the Revd Christopher Couperthwaite died Aged 78 after been 52 years Vicar of Dalton
30 begun to set our potatos

May

6 begun to Sow Barley had done on the 10 May
18 Laid our young Cattle out
19 Betty Batersby Interd aged 72

Jun

4 laid our Milk cows out
18 Thos Ashburner of Bridgegate Died aged 69
26 Begun to Mow our seed Grass

July

3 Begun to Mow our Meddows Augt 6 had got all our Medow hay
9 Laid our Horses out||

Aug

3 R Geldard came to Spend the Day with us
17 Mrs Parker & her son with Margt Garnett & Mr Whinram from Ulverston came to Dine & spend the Day with us at Barrow
30 begun to Shear Septr 25th Shore out

Sept

14 My Wife & I went Spend the Day at Redmain Hall with Robt Chatburn Geldart[14]

Octr

12 had done Housing all our Grain after a very tedious Season
20 Laid our Milk Cows in
17 Betty Cragg Died relect of Wm Cragg late of Barrow aged 49 years
21 Richd Simpson of Dalton was drowned on Duddon Sands whilst fishing aged 40 years
22 begun to sow Wheat had done on the 31 Oct
29 laid our Two Mares in the House

Decr

4 a very heavy Storm of wind & rain Blew our house doer penthous down and apart of the parlor Chimne top off
13 begun to Plow, had done March 13 1824
25 John Bolton of North Scale Died aged 35 years

1824

Feby

4 Joseph Fisher Daughter Isabella died aged 8 Months
26 Mr Thos Park commited to Lancaster Castle Thos Kendals Servant girl having Swore a Rape against him

March

14 Thos Park aquitted by the Grand jurey at Lancaster Castle
14 Margt Garnett of Ulverston Died aged 76 years
16 a Child Burnd to Death in Kirkby in the absence of its Mother
17 a barn Burnd down at Gleaston the Fire originated by some Sparks from a smiths shop agoining the Building
29 begun to Sow Oats had done on the 9 April
31 the Ground covered with Snow & hard frost

April

22 begun to Set Potatos
Ellener Bland of Lyth Married to Daniel Hodgshon Grocer of Wthaven on the 12 April

May

8 begun to Sow Barly had done on the 18th May
17 Willm Gibson of North Scale in Walney Died very suddenly aged 68 years
22 Laid our young cattle out 29 Laid our Milch Cows out

June

12 begun to cut our Seed Grass
23 Laide Britton out
30 Margt Wilkinson Died aged 43||

July

5 Laid our Horses out
13 I went to Thos Bows Sheep Shearing
13 begun to Mow our Medow Ground 23 had got all our Medow hay
25 Rob Geldard John Parker & George Whinram came to Dine and Spend the Day with us at Barrow
30 I went to Kendal and found all Freands well

Augst

7 George Fell Married to Ellen Walton of North Scale Island of Walney
12 Begun to Shear Shore out 18 Septr
15 my Wife & myself went to Spend the day with Mr & Mrs Lesh at Hollowmire we also meet James & Betty Butcher from Cocken & a Miss Wilson from Lyth Near Kendal

Septr

21 begun to sow Wheat 28 had done except the Potato ground
25 Thos Park of Ulverstoe Married to Ann Fisher Daughter of Joseph Fisher of Barrow Aged 18 years
30 Had done housing all our Grain

Octr

18 I was summoned to the Sessons at Lancaster[15]
24 laid our Milk Cows in Do 25 laid Smiler in
25 Richd Lowder of Roosecoat Died aged 80 years

Novr

6 Laid our young Cattle in 9 Laid Strngr & Britton in
24 Thos Fresh Married to Margt Robinson of Newbarns
25 Wm Creary of Billin Coat Interd aged 70 years Died on the 22nd inst.

28 George Case of Pees Holms with his sister Brother in Low and Sister Miss Wright of Ramside & a Miss Jonson of Liverpool Came to spend the afternoon with us was a very wet & sormey Day
29 Christopher Simpson Died aged 91 years
Died on the 14 Novr Mr John Simpson late an Officer in his Majestys Customs at Barrow aged 72 years

Decr

13 John Berry of Rampside Tide Surveyor of the Customs of Pile Fouldrey Died on the 13 of Decr 1824 aged 52 years[16]
27 Died on the 27 John Lewthwaite of Newtown near Rampside aged 84 years||

1825

Jany

1 Thomas Postlethwaite of Hawcoat Married
10 Begun to Plow
17 Thos Bows Daughter Mary Died of the Tyhs [typhus] Fever aged 11 years
21 awfully sudden at Dalton Margret Hartley Daughter of John Hartley aged 25 years she was found Dead in her bed
31 a sloope Calld the Aurora about 30 Tons Burden was wrecked below South-end [Walney] and all on Board Perrishd the men wear washed on Shore Soown afterwards and one of them had 36 soverins with the Vessels papers in his Pocket another had a watch. the belonged to Preston

Feby

21 Thos Kellet of Salthous Died aged 76 years
22 Edward Park Cockin Died after a long Illiness aged 57
Married at Ulversto on the 15 Feby by the Revd J. Sunderland A. M. Phillip B. Dean Esq to Agness youngest daughter of the late Roger Kilner Esqr

March

20 a large Timber ship was discharged at Barrow about this time.
24 begun to sow Oats had done on the 31 avery fine season never knew the ground work better

April

21 finished Setting Potatos

May

9 begun to Sow Barley had done on the 16
15 My Wife & me with Brother John & Mary went to Dine and Spend the Day at Billing Coat

16 Laid our young Cattle out Do 22 Laid our Milk Cows out

18 John Case of Dalton Died aged [?]

27 had a verry heavy Hale Showr avery could Sharp wind on the 28

June

4 Jane Coward of Little Mill Married to Wm Tiks of Millom

7 Wm Kendal of Salthous Married to Jane Phizaklea of Walney||

19 Laid our horses out

18 begun to Cut our Seed grass July 4 had done Housing Do [ditto]

July

5 Begun to Cut our Medow Grass had Cut all our Meddow Grass on 12

10 Robt Geldart Mrs Barker & her son George Whinram Robt Smith and his wife Mary Creary & Richd Creary wife [crossed out 'her daughter in Low'] came to Dine and Spend the Day with us at Barrow

had the Newsepaper Calld the Sunday times on the 30 June

19 had got all our Meddow hay the 2 or 3 suckeding days was the Hottest I ever remembered we got 72 Cart Lods of hay

Augst

6 Begun to Shear Shore out 2 September

My Wife & Son Richd and James went to Lyth and Kendal on the 29 July & returned on the 2 August

Strainger was 5 years old in the Summer of 1825

Britten was 4 years old in the Summer of 1825[17]

the first Kendal paper came on Thursday 21 July

31 had done housing all our Oats Septr 8 had done housing Barly

Septr

16 Begun to Sow Wheat had done on the 1 October having a verry good Season

17 my Wife and I went to Pennybridge to see John Dixon returned on the 18

24 Died on the 24 Thos Kendal of Salthous after a lingering Illiness aged 51 years

29 had got all our Potaton

Octr

13 Newsepaper 2r Due paid Mr Knipe 3/- [three shillings]

24 Laid Strainger in the House Do [ditto] Our Milk Cows

22 Ellen Myres of Seaflatend was Killed by a Tup [a ram] whilst passing through a field betwixt Holebeck and Rooscoat She was found dead upon the spot and was very much brused about the head and arms she was 76 years of Age

30 My Wife & John went Dine and Spend the day with Robt Geldart at redmain Hall we met there the Revnd Wm Ashburner and the Revd J, Ponsonby Mrs Parker & her son Mr & Mrs Stamper and Miss Crewson from Ulverston & Mrs Thomas Coward from Couppark||

Novr

3 laid our Horses in the house
6 A brig Called the Susana of Whitehaven was Wrecked on the West side of the Island of Walney and all on Board Perished she was in ballast
23 George Pressa [Presow] of Sunbrick put a period to his existance by hanging himself no cose could be assind for the rash act he was upward of 70 years of Age

Decr

25 Richard Gardner of Newbarns departed this life in is the 76th year
26 four of our Relations from Holm near Burton in Kendal came To spend a few days with us & returned on the 30
31 Thos & Margret Bows came to see us

1826

Jany

7 begun to Plow begun to frees same night
9 George Hoole of Newton Died Aged 76 years

Feby

11 Alice Cragg Daughter of the Late Wm and Elizabeth Cragg Died after along Indispotion which she bore with Christian fortidue and resignation aged 27 years
16 Married at Lancaster James Satterthwaite Esqr of that place to Miss Hughes granddaughter of Thos Edmondson Esqr of Grass yard Hall Caton

March

15 Margt Fisher wife of Richd Fisher of Lancester Merchant Departed this life much respected aged 46 years[18]
23 Begun to Sow Oats had done 4 April

April

10 Miss Fell of Red-main Hall Died aged 92 years

May

6 Finished Setting Potatos begun to Sow Barley
11 had done sowing Barley
13 laid our young Cattle out 20 Laid our Milk Cows out

June

10 Laid our Horses out
14 begun to Mow our Seed Grass 20 begun to Mow our medows
29 had done mowing our Medwos [sic] July 3 got all our Meddow Hay||

July

8 I went to Thos Bows Sheep Shearing with Mary Richd and Wm James also Brother John & his Wife returnd on 10th

11 Woman Killd at Dendron by falling from a cart Load of Hay her name was Elizabeth Lewthwaite aged 62

24 Margret Jackson of Leece Deparded this Life aged 83 years
begun to shear on the 22 July shore out Augst 18th

27 a little girl of Robt Kendals of Barrow having been sent from the shearing field for a piece of fire to light her grandmothes pipe was so dreadfully burned that she died a few days afterwards it is supposed she had covered the fire with a part of her dress and in running it had ignited; she was with her grandmother at Newland near Ulverston

Septr

1 had got all our Grain Housed

12 begun to Sow Wheat 16 had done all but 3 rigs & 2 rigs Head
On the 6 Septr the Town of Ulverston Captn Hewetson was Lost near Liverpool the crew and twelve passengers all Perished, also the same night the Royal Oak Captn Dickinson of Ulverston, the hands with some Passengers all Perished

Octr

3 had got all our Potatos

20 plowed High Close for Barley fallow

30 Laid our Milch Cows in

31 Laid Strainger in

1827

Jany

2 Laid Br [Briton] & Smiler in house

16 Begun to Plow 25 March had done Plowing

March [*sic*]

26 Begun to sow Oats||

Feby

14 Mathew Coward of Little Mill Died aged 72 years

17 Thos Bows brought me 4 Bushl Oats from Fenwick for Seed he had a deal of Snow as he came averry hard frost and keen wind the next day

25 James Kendal of Salthous died aged 82 years

March

Thomas Sowerbuts killd at the Iorn Ore pits by the roof of the pit falling in

23 A vessel 70 tons burthen Called the Commers Oliver Haddock Master belonging to Ulverston with 200 Barels of Gun powder on Board 10 Tons weight bound to Liverpool, laying near Ramside by some means the vessel got on fire which soon got to the powder went of with dreadful Explosion the hands had time to get away from her the report was felt very forsebly in Lancaster Garstang and Preston

April

5 begun to Sow Oats had done on the 14th
10 had done Setting potatos
12 Begun to Sow Barley had [done] on the 19 May
13 Laid our young Cattle Out

[*May*]

Mr Robert Turner of Lyth near Kendal Died on the 7 May 1827 aged 77 years

June

10 Laid our Horses out
20 Thos Brockbank son of Thos Brockbank of Salthous Died aged 11 years
23 begun to Cut our seed Grass
28 Thos Walton of Old Barrow Died of the Typhus Fever aged 41 years

July

7 begun to Cut our Meddow Grass
8 Brother John Richd & Wm James & myself went to Tho Bows Clipping
15 my Wife & I went to Dine & spend the Day with Robt Geldard at Redmain Hall and met there the Reved Wm Ashburner Mr & Mrs Stamper Miss Crewson Mr & Mrs Couper of Scales Mr & Mrs Ashburner of Do [ditto] Mr & Mrs Winder of Do Mr & Mrs Gold of rooscoat & Mr Batersby of Lindle My Wife begun to be very poorly & was Obliged to retire from the Company and Lay down

Augt

11 begun to Shear Had done on Septr 8 had done Housing 22 Sepr

Septr

18 begun to sow Wheat had done on the 25 Septr

Octr

8 had done getting Potatos||
18 laid Strainger in Do [ditto] 22 laid our Milk Cows in

Decr

31 Robt Chatburn Geldart of redman Hall Married to Ann Couper of Scales

1828

Jan

21 Begun to Plow

Feby

8 Died at Ulverston Mr James Coward Mercer and Draper aged 31 leaving a widow and two children to deplor the loss of a kind husband and an affectionate father

14 Mathew Dobson of Hawcoat was lost in Crossing Walney Meetings [a ford] in a dreadful Snow Storm (and was not found on the 3 March)

Mar

19 Iabella Bowes Wife of John Bowes LadyHall departed this life (in childbed) aged 44 years

26 Begun to sow Oats had done on the 8 April

April

6 (Easter Sunday) My Brother Richd Fisher & two of his Daughters Margt & Elizabeth paid us a Visit (from Lancaster) previous to thier going to Liverpool to reside. Yesterday Miss Forster Miss Clark & Mr Jno Parker also Paid us a visit for the Day. And Thomas Bowes arrived in the evening.
Myself Br Richd Thos Bowes My Daughters Margt & Mary with Margt & Elizabeth Fisher (my son Richd also) all went to see Furness Abby & retd to Tea John Fisher was also of the party

19 Richd Fell of Biggar in the Island of Walney Married to Margret Atkinson of Dalton

19 William Harrinson House reared[19]

May

8 Begun to sow Barley had Done on the 20 May

10 Begun to Set Potatos
Died on the 24 April Robt Thornton of North Scale in the Island of Walney Aged 89 years

20 Mr William Townson of Furness Abby Died aged 73 years

26 John Heslam of Hindpool Married to . . . Smith of Cartmell

27 Captr Thos Mattix of the Ship Mary of Ulverston Married to Mary Harrinson Daughter of Thos Harrinson of Barrow, she was just turnd of 17 years of Age||

28 George Huddleston servant man to Joseph Fisher Married to Mary Hunter Daughter of the late Mathew Hunter of Dalton

28 Laid out Milch Cows out

June

1 Died at Ulverston Mr Robt Town aged 72 for many years one of the most respectable tradesmen in that place and held in general estimation as an upright an honourable man[20]

9 Died at Dalton Mathew Denney aged 69 years
12 a child of the name of Pool was killd at Dalton by a fall from a saw pit aged 9 years John Noble was married to Margt Stable of Hawcoat on the 6 June
13 got a swarm of Bees 17 begun to Cut our seed Grass
21 laid our Horses Out
27 Begun to Cut our Meddow Grass and got all our Medow Hay July 17

July

5 Richd, Wm James, John Eliza and myself went to Thos Bows Sheep Shearing, returnd on the 6th

Augt

11 begun to Shear Shore out on the 5 Septr
Died in the prime of life in June Mrs Mary Turner wife of Wm Turner of Lyth near Kendal
6 James Barrow son of Captn Barrow fell from the Quay in concequence of a rail giving way which he was leaning against he lingered in great agoney till the 22 when he expired aged 19 years
24 Died at Dalton Christopher the youngest son of the late Revd C. Couperthwaite aged 24

Sept

1 Died at Dalton John Stable maney years Clerk and Sexton of Dalton Church aged 46
9 Ann Parker died after a lingering Illness aged 64
11 a daughter of John Heslams of Bigger Died in Child bed of the Types feever
29 the Brig Mary Captn Mattex belonging to Ulverston laden with Grain from Irland to Southhamton|| was upset in a sudden Gale of wind and soon after went down in 30 fathoms Water with 3 of her unfortunate Crew out of Seven the Captn and 3 others was taken up by a small fishing Boat one Old man Died in the Boat before the got to shore the Axident took place at place called Howeth head in Irland not fare from Dublin

Octr

18 James MacKreth Married to Ann Dixon
24 laid Strainger in

Nov

15 George Pressa of North Scale in the Island of Walney Married to Elizabeth Daughter of Joseph Fisher of Barrow
Do Thos Turner of Dalton to Mary Danson of Hawcoat
Do John Hudson to Frances Gibson Daughter of the late Wm Gibson of North Scale in the Island of Walney
25 James Benson of Ireleth & John Brockbank of Dalton wear Sufacated by the foul air at Crosgates Iorn Ore pit [near Lindal] there was two others in at the same time which escaped with dificulty by accinding the Shaft in the bucket both the unfortnate men have left widdows and small famileys to bewail there loss

Decr

21 John Elliot of Ulverston Died aged 61 years
24 Ester the Daughter of John Bows junr of Lady hall Died aged 22 years

1829

Jany

12 Willm Bolton of Parkhous Died aged 30 years

Feby

6 Died at North Scale Island of Walney the wife of Robt Greenwood aged 68 years

March

12 George Case Married to Margret Wright of Ramside
30 Begun to Sow Oats had done 7 April

April

1 a heavy hail showre the weather very moderat it went off before noon

May

2 had Done setting potatos||
9 Begun to sow Barley had done on the 14 May
18 Jane Siks of Salthous in Cumberland [near Millom] Interd at Dalton she was daughter to the late Mathew and Margt Coward of Little Mill she died in Childbed aged 36 yeary
26 laid our Milch Cows out
16 A child about 7 years old the daughter of John Jackson of Leece, was so sevearly crushed by a roller that after experience the greatest pain she expired on the Wedensday following it is a very remarkable as well as unfortunate circumstance that Dr Couperthwaite of Dalton, should have fractured a leg upon the preceding night, about the same place and was laid upon the same bed (from whence he was only removed in the morning) where John Jacksons child, whose leg was also fractured, was taken to, and upon which she expired.
24 a cow house and granery was burned down at Manner the Cattle was saved with Great difficulty as the Strow was burning before there heads it was suposed that some hot ashes had been laid two near the Bulding so had set the strow on fire

June

1 a sloop calld the Venox belonging to Cardigan got upon the Loding bank and the tide Ebbing she could not be got off again she went down on her Brode side and was not got up again till the 3rd there was verry little damage done
9 Doctor Allen late of Dalton was interd at Ulverston Aged 33 years
24 laid our Horses out & begun to Cut our Seed Grass

July

18 had done getting hay out of Medows

Augt

5 went to Kendal returned on the 6
5 begun to Shear had done on 16 Septr
had done Housing 28 September||

Oct

2 Begun to Sow Wheat had done on the 7
7 Black Comb Topt with Snow[21]
9 Had done Getting Potatos
3 foundation stone of a new Church at Ulverston was laid by John Bolton[22] Esqr of Storrs hall,—the followin Inscription was deposseted under neath it . . . A bottle containing several coins and a written scroll was deposited in a cavity prepared for its reception over which a brass plate bearing the following inscription:– 'On this Site given by Henry Low Esqr of Ulverston the first stone of a new Church to be didicated to the holy Trinity was laid on the 3 Octr 1829 in the tenth year of the reign of King George IV by John Bolton Esqr of Storrs Hall; T.R.G. Braddyll Esqr Lay Rector the Revr John Sunderland A.M. Incumbent'
18 laid Strainger in Do 19 Laid our Milch Cows in
the word AND: occurs in the Old and New Testament 46, 227 times the word Jehovah occurs 6, 855 times Ezra 7. 21 contains the whole Alphbet 2nd Kings Chapter 19 and Isaiah Chapter 37 are alike[23]

Decr

24 Agnes Fell of Newton Died aged 51 years
25 James Harrinson of Newbarns Died aged 91 years

1830

Similies I hope I don't intrud'—as the knife said to the oyster "come in" as the spider said to the fly "come on" as the man said to his tight boot "you can make me blush"—as the lobster cried out in the saucepan Mirror
Died on the 7 March at Ulverston Mr Wm. Daws iron founder aged 50 he bore a protracted illness with the greatest fortitude and resignation and died lamented by his numerous friends and acquaintance||

March

12 George Robinson of Dalton died of the small pox aged 27
29 begun to sow Oats had done on the 6 April
22 March Mr James Picthall school master married to Mrs Margret Munchaster Confectnor Both of Ulverston[24]

April

1/2 hard frost we could no Harrow in the fornoon 3r all Covered with snow but went off before noon

6 Richd Machel Esqr of Ulverston died aged 85 years

12 Wm Denney of Low field house died aged 38 years

14 a servant girl of the name of Winder was Killed by a threshing Machen at Winder Hall in Cartmell

May

1 Wm Harrinson Married to Elizabeth Huddelston

12 Begun to sow barley had done on the 19 May

20 had Done Setting Potatos

23 John Rowel of Holebeck died aged 60 years

June

1 Miss Walker of North Scale in the Island of Walney Married to a Mr Strich from Liverpool

23 begun to cut our Seed Grass

July

3 begun to Cut our Meddows had done getting medows 27 July

10 went to Thos Bows Sheep Shearing returned on the 12

12 King William 4th Proclamed at Dalton

15 King George 4th Buried

29 Jacob Parker tide surveyor[25] at Barrow died aged 56 he was Interd at Kirkby Church by Mr Pearson aged 81 years

Aug

7 I went to Kendal and returned on 9 found all Friends well

18 begun to Shear Septr 21 Shore out

Septr

21 Tho Dilworth[26] died aged 40 year leaving 9 childer and Pregnant Widdow to Deplore his loss

Octr

5 had done Housing all our Grain||

the Right Honourable Wm Huskisson Died 15 September in his 61st year of his age AD 1830 his Death was cosed by one of the Steam Ingens going over his leg and thigh at the Opening of the Liverpool and Manchester railway

3 Myls Coward a young man Hanged himself at Swartmore Hall he was Son to John Coward of Windle no cose could be assigned for the rash act

11 Begun to sow Wheat had done on the 16

15 had done getting Potatos
21 Laid our Milch Cows in the house
23 Laid Strainger in

Nov

2 Thos Chark of Ulverston Died in the 91th year of his age

Decr

12 Betty Lowther of Rooscoat Died Interrd 15 aged 75 years
A boy about 10 years Old Son of John Picthall of Holmbank Near Much Urswick was Drowned Whilst Skating on a tarn near Urswick Church in Jany 1830[27]

1831

March

23 had done plowing
22 John Gardner of Denderon died aged 85 years
28 begun to sow Oats had done on the 5 April a dry season

April

2 John Kilner Park son of Thos Park of Millwood died aged 5 months
18 Peter Buttler Mercer and Draper Ulverston married to Margret Fisher daughter of Joseph Fisher of Barrow the bride was 17 years old
26 had done setting Potatos
27 George Stamper a servant man was Struck at by a Horse whilst the wear showing at Broughton fair and died the following Day

May

4 Begun to plow Barley had done on the 10 a very Dry Season
17 Betty Wilkinson died at Pennybridge and was Intered at Walney Chaple on the 20 aged 87 years
18 Betty Stuart died at Dalton in her 105th year
18 George Fell Daughter Margret Married to John Postlethwaite of Low House in Cumberland on the 14th May
28 laid our Milch cows out||

June

6 Laid our Horses out
13 A young man named Wm Crayston of Scales Park in Low Furness was unfortunately drowned whilst bathing near Aldingham

July

2 went to Thos Bows sheep shearing found them all well begun to cut our medow grass July 1 had cut all our medows 12

10 My wife and I went to spend the day with Mr and Mrs Greenwood at North scale in Walney and met there Mr and Mrs Geldard of Redman Hall and Mr Denny of Dalton
18 finished our Meddow Hay very thin crop
28 Begun to Shear Shore out on the 27 August a very fine Harvest the Greatest part of the Grain was secured by the end of August escept Barley that was rather back finished Housing 3 Septr

Aug

21 Robt Crearey fought with a man of the name of Readhead at Dalton one Sunday in harvest he Died on the Thursday following a Coronor Inquest was held before Wm Blendal Esqr and a Virdit of Mans Slaughter was brought in against Readhead who absconded Crearey was the beginer of the fight and cleared Readhead of any blame before he Died

Sepr

24 Robt Nicklson Died of a Pluresy Fever aged 55 years
24 Willm Harrinson Tide Surveyer Died at Kirkby aged 70 years
24 Joseph Fisher of Dalton Married to Dina Wilimanson
30 Begun to sow wheat had done 4 Octr

Octr

13 Laid Strainger in Do 21 Br [Briton] laid in Octr 22 Laid our Cows in

Novr

5 Thos Danson of Hawcoat Died aged 77
10 Mr Robt Fell of Ulverston Died many years Banker in that Town aged 79 years
13 Died Mrs Jane Gibson widdow of the late William Gibson of Northscale in the Island of Walney aged 75 years
Died on the 21 October Marey Cockerton daughter of George Cockerton of Dalton she fell down whilst dressing and Expired Immeadtly aged 44 years—the above was omitted setting down in its proper place
19 Thos Hartley married to Ester Slater Both of Dalton||

1832

Jany

3 Betty Bows Died aged 60 years She died at Bank end near Duddon bridg and was Interd at Whates Chaple [Hallthwaites]
13 Elizabeth Harrinson Recclect of James Harrinson of Barrow Died after a lingerins sickness aged 87
14 Elizabeth James Wife of Joseph James of Kirby Irleth Died aged 52 years
15 James Kellet [of Salthouse] casterated himself
17 John Gibson from Liverpool left our House after Spending a forthnight with us

19 A Child of Simeon Thwaits stone mason about 4 years Old was so Dreadfully burnd by its close taking Fire in the Abcence of its mother to fetch some water that it died in a few hours afterwards.

Feby

5 Mark Simpson Shot himself the ball entered is Bowels he lived about 12 Hours after he was a man that was much adicted to Drinking and it is suposed that he had done it in a fit of Tempery deraingement he lived at Ulverston

13 had done Plowing

March

24 begun to Sow Beans 26 sowed my Skinless Oats & Boling Pees and a little Potato Oats all in Whins April 3 had done sowing Oat

23 John Wilson of Lindle was killd by a fall from his Horse as he was returning from Ulverston

April

16 had done Setting Potatos a very dry season

May

7 begun to Sow Barley had done on the 16 May
Margt Bows died on the 24 April aged 24 years

26 Got a swarm of Bees had a 2nd swarm 10 days after

June

10 Got another swarm of Bees 2nd swarm 11 days after

27 got another fore swarm
begun to Cut our Seed Grass on the 21 June

July

6 John Parker died aged 55 years Old

23 had got all our Meddow Hay with verry fine Weather||

Aug

8 Begun to shear Septr 11 Shore out

9 a boy of Richd Postlethwaites of Leece was Killd by falling out of a cart in going from Ulverston Market

10 Ann Mawson Wife of Moses Mawson Dyer of Ulverston was Burned to Death by her Close taking fire it was suposed that she had falen down in a fit

15 a son of Thos Sharp of Cocken about 12 years of age was going to Angerton Moss it was thought that he had dropped alseep on the Cart head and fallen of and the Wheel and the hinder horse had gone over him he only lived till the next Morning
Died on the 7 Aug James Robinson of Newbarns aged 32

Octr

2 begun to sow Wheat had done on the 3rd
6 James Fell Married to Mary Kendal of Stank
15 Mary Walton Married to James Holm
15 Georg Simpson died aged 68 years
24 John Bolton of Parkhous Married to Miss Coward of Newbiggin

Novr

17 John Paxton [of Biggar] had a stack of hay burnd there is no doubt but it had been set of fire by some Incendry a man of the name of Charnock was taken up upon suspision but the could not bring suffient proof to convict him but still he was thought Guilty

Decr

2 Thos Boltons house[28] was struck by Litining which Broke 9 Windows to attoms and shatterd the pump box and Melted the Lead the damage was estimated at about 30 pound there was no person Hurt tho there was several of the family in the Kitchin at the time it happened
Joseph Walton of Northscale Island of Walney Married to Ann Hudelston of Rooscoat daughter of Thos Huddelston of the same place on 26 Novr 1832||
30 Thomas Harrinson of Barrow died Aged 62 years

1833

Jany

1 Elizabeth Atkinson of Dalton Married to Wm Hudelston of rooscoat

March

13 had done Plowing
19 begun to Sow Beans Do 22 begun to sow Oats Had done sowing Oats I never knew the Land work so kindly in my 40 years expearience April 1 1833
30 Betty Fell Daughter of James Fell Married to Thos Coulton otherwise Myers otherwise Hunter

April

30 had done setting Potatos

May

4 Begun to Sow Barley May 9 had done sowing Barley

June

18 Begun to Cut our Seed Grass 5 July had it all housed we had a sever Gale of wind accompanied with heavy rain on the 11 June which drove several Vessels from their moornings at Piel one laden with salt got so much damaged that she sunk but was near the Shore the salt all melted out of her and it is doubted whether she will be fit to repair again or not

18 amanks [Manx] Fishing Boat it was an Open Boat was also lost with 5 men on board to the west of Walney Isle 3 of them are washed on shore at the time I write this June 19 the other 2 also was found and all interd at Walny Chapple

July

6 begun to cut our Meddow Grass

6 Thos Bows sheep shearing

Aug

8 Begun to shear Shore out 10 Sept 19 had done Shearing Beans

13 Sarah Robinson Married to Henry Case

31 Wm Greenwood of Northscale in the Island of Walney Died aged 80 years

Sep

30 Lenord Gould of Rooscoat Died verry suddenly he was sitting in a Neighbours House he fell out of His Chair and Expired Immediatly aged 76 years

Octr

1 Ann Hartley relect of the late Pillap Hartley of Dalton Died aged 76 years||

7 Begun to sow wheat had done 11 sowed Potato Land with Wheat 2nd Novr in near More [Near Moor]

8 a young woman aged about 19 of the name—Jackson hanged herself in a barn at Peesholms

On the 7 Octr a child about 14 Months Old was Scalded to Death a girl having let it fall into a panful of Boiling Water at Anker near Lindle

Decr

24 2 men killed at Kirkby Slate Quarrys by a Quantity of rubish falling upon them both have left famelys to deplore there untimly fate of there only supporters

24 On the same day a man was instantaneously killed and a nother seriously injured that his life is dispared of at the Backbarrow acid works near Ulverston[29]

31 On the 31 Decr we had a heavy Gale of Wind which drove the schooner Iris of Wthaven from her moorings and through the high end of the Old Quay till with 10 feet of Josephs Fisher Gardin wall the same vessel and two others was drove on shore behind the Ile of Walney aboute five Weeks before in a simmler Gale, one of them an Irish Brig and the other a Duch Galliot the wear all three partly loden with salt and all got of again but most part of the salt was lost

1834

March

4 we had done plowing for oats

11 Mary the wife of Joseph Fisher of Barrow fetched to Ulverston to see her Daughter Margaret Buttler who was at the point of Death and when they arrived she had breathed her last[30] Mary was taken ill and expired in a few Hours they wear both interd in one grave in Dalton church yard on the 14 Mary aged 47 and Margaret her daughter aged 20 years

21 Begun to sow Beans 31 begun to sow Oats had done 7 April

31 Ann Kendal wife of John Kendal of Newbarns died of the Typhes fever aged 44 leaving six small childer

begun to sow Barley 2nd May had done on the 13th

May

1 Mr Thos Garnett of Dalton departed this life aged 71 he filld the Situation of headmaster to the free Grammar school of that place for [Blank] years and died much Lamented and respected by all who had the pleasure of his aquantance||

July

1 John Stephenson of Nettleslack Married to Isabella Brockbank of Salthous she was brot to bed 26 Octr folling

12 Mr Pemberton of Pegebank died 84 years

John Parker of Ulverston married to Elizabeth Brathwaite of Grathwaite near Hawkshead on 10 May 1834

June

22 James Gibson of Dalton Interd he had been about 50 years Black Smith of that place aged 78 years

July

24 Ann Gibson Widdow of the above James Gibson Died aged 75 years

Augst

10 William Barker of Barrow died aged 77 years

14 Aggnes Case of Dalton Widdow of John Case late of Furness Abbey died aged 77 years

We begun to Shear on the 7th Aug and shore out on the 27 Shearers 4/– & 3/6 per day owing to so maney being wanted the Harvest comenced in all parts of the Country at the same time[31] Wheat and this year is afaling Crop particularly in the Island of Walney and money other places it was quite washed of in Winter and obliged to be sown with Oats in the spring and from the wetness of the Weather of late Wheat will be sadly sprouted I writ this on the 31 Aug

Augt

23 Robt Ashburner of Ulverston died much respected
24 Elizabeth Forster of Ulverston died 71 years

Septr

13 had done Housing after a very wet Season

Octr

2 had done Getting potatos
6 begun to sow wheat had done on the 8 a verry fine season
21 Laid our cows in 22 laid Br [Briton] in

Octr

Elizabeth the wife of Nickler Fisher of Little Mill Stile[32] begun in the Cholera on the night of the 7 and died on the 8 her Grand Daughter residing with her begun on the 12 and died on the 13th Nicholas Fisher husband of the above Elizabeth Fisher begun on the 14 and died on the 15 a Daughter took it afew days after but recovered again it threw the Contrey in to such an alarm it was thought nessary to prevent is farther spreading to burn every article in the House the Clock alone was saved and it had the desired effect. I write this Decr 22 and there has not been another Case the loss will be mad up by the Parish||

1835

Feby

5 a Manks smack Laden with Wheat was drove on shore on Fouley Island near Ramside the Capt and a yound girl about 8 years of age a passenger Perrished thro the inclemance of the weather after the got on shore the wear bound to Liverpool

March

24 begun to sow beans
30 begun to sow oats had done 11 April

May

8 begun to sow Barley had done 26 wet season
17 James Heslam son of Thos Heslam Talor died aged 22
23 John Jackson of Leece Married to Mary Kendal of Cockel scare

June

16 Laid our horses out 17 begun to cut our seed Grass

July

3 begun to Cut our Meddows
4 myself Richd & John went to Thos Bows sheep Shearing found them all well returned on the next day
20 Mowed our long rean Meddow had all the Hay howesed on the 24

Aug

19 Begun to shear Shore out 12 Septr shearers wags 4s 3/6 2/6 and 2s p day
14 Wm Danson of Hawcoat Died aged 84 years
20 a shock of an Earthquake was felt here and for 20 Mile distant
21 a child about 2 years Old of Lish Scots of Dalton was drowned in one of the Tan pits in the absence of Its mother
do 4 cows and a pig was killd by the Lighting at Broughton in Furness

Sept

4 Mils Gibson of Northscale Island of Walney died with only a few hours sicknes aged 58 years
19 had done shearing beans 27 had done Howsing Beans
Wm Bolton of Bridge Gate Died the 17 Septr aged 73

Octr

1 Mr John Watson of Cumberland land surveyor married to Miss Elliner Rowlendson of Kendal
10 Anty High of Leece died aged 71
19 had done getting Potatos 22 had done sowing Wheat
23 laid our Cows in do laid Billy in

Decr

12 William Walker of Northscale Island of Walney died aged 22 years
21 Begun to plow||

1836

Jany

29 a child of T. Hodgson Cost Tide water Died aged about 6 Months Interd at Walney without any serimony being of the Romen perswason[33]
30 Wm Ashburner son of George Ashburner of Elliscales died aged 14 years

Feby

6 Sarah Creary wife of Wm Creary of Marton died aged 39 years

March

18 Wm Gleave of Lancaster Died aged [?]
24 Begun to sow Beans had done on the 26

April

1 James Hunter wife of Urswick hanged herself
1 George Martins House of Ramside was Burned down nothing was saved except 5 Chairs and a few Bed Cloth the famley Escapd in a state of Nudity it is suposed that it was the work of some Incendry
9 Begun to Sow Oats had done on the 19 a very wet season
18 Ellen Fisher Daughter of Joseph Fisher married to Richd Cornthwaite of Cartmell

May

4 Begun to sow Barley had done on the 13
18 had done setting potatos
22 Elizabeth Kellett of Salthouse died aged 85 years

June

1 Laid our Milk cows out
7 a boy of Wm Atkinsons of Lindle was thrown from a horse and Killd upon the spot
10 Philip Hartley son of John and Betty Hartley of Barrow Died Aged 2 years
15 Laid our Horses out
25 begun to cut our seed Grass

July

1 begun to Cut our Meddow Grass
1 Mary Garnett Daughter of John and Mary Garnett of Ulverston Died with an inflamation in the Bowers aged 25 years
9 Brother John and son John went to Thos Bows sheep shearing
19 Sarah Heslam daughter of Thos Heslam Died after a lingering Illness aged 21 years||

Aug

22 begun to shear Shore out Barly 4 Octr Do shore out Beans 17 Oct
22 John Woodburn Hodgson Captn of the Hope of Ulverston drowned in going from Barrow to his Vessel at poolfoot he was in a state of Intoxication he was a man very much respected in his situation and not much Inclined to getting toow much drink

Septr

3 Betty Atkinson Daughter of William and Ester Atkinson Died aged 17 years
4 William Simpson of Barrow Died aged 71 years

Octr

18 Begun to sow Wheat had done on the 28
25 laid our cows in Novr 2 laid Bl and St in

Novr

29 a child of Robt Harrinson of Hawcoat was Burnd to death by its Close taking fire whlst its Mother was gone to fetch some water about 3 years Old

4 housed the latter end of our Beans

12 Thos Nelson Married to Cathran Postlethwaite Daughter of Thos Postlethwaite of Hawcoat

26 Betty Kitchin Wife of John Kitchin of Irleth and Daughter of James Fisher of Dalton died in child bed aged 29 years

27 Betty Kendle wife of James Kendal of Dalton painter and Glasier Died in Child bed aged 26 years

Dec

19 Thos Addinson of Hawcoat died aged 92 years

1837

Jany

17 begun to plow

Narrow escape on the 14th Jany Antoney Smith Black smith at Lindle went to Scale bank to Invite a young man to a dance the young man foolishly took up agun with a view of frightining him and pointing it within a few yards it went off and the whole charge struck Anthony Smith on or about the breast at first Instant death seemd inevitable|| but it was not so bad as mite be expected he recovered in about fourteen days the youth who fired the gun was unconscious of its being loaded but it out to be awarning to all never to tamper with human life by sporting with fatal weapons

19 Fatal accident on Duddon Sands William Clark of Barfield and Robt James a neighbour wear comming to Ulverston Market the Morning being verry dark the got lost on the sands the shouted and the wear heard to Marchgraings a man rode down and found Clark and his Horse fast in the Quick Sand and tide flowing the could not get too him the got a Boat he was got off horse but died soon after the horse was dead under him Robt James was found in the same place the next day it is suposed that he had fallen from his horse at the time it went in to the hole the Horse got out alive

Feby

6 Thos Coward of Newbiggin Married to Mary Bolton of Bridgegate her sister Mrs Ashburner of Eliscales was brought to bed on the same day

March

4 Ann Barker Died aged 78 years

7 John Bows of Fennwick near Broughton Died 91 years

8 Wm King of Moss side Died aged 43 years

11 John Hartley of Dalton Died aged 73 years

20 Begun to sow beans 24 begin to sow Oats

22 Miss Richardson of Old Park near Ireleth died aged 74 years
29 Mathew Coward Miller of Green in Cumberland Died aged 55 he was eldest son of the late Mathew Cowerd of Little Mill near Dalton in Furness
30 Wm Slater of Sourby Lodge Died aged 80 years

April

11 finished sowing Oats never knew the Land work so well in general it was very frosty in the Mornings||
7 died at Ulverston Mr James Picthall Iorn Founder aged 43 years
21 a son of Wm Robinsons of Barrow died aged 5 years and 6 months
24 begun to sow Barley had done 6 of May had done setting potatos 9

May

2 Elizabeth Robinson of New barns died aged 81 years
9 the ground covered with snow but soon went off
11 Henrey Robinson son of Wm & Rachel Robinson of Barrow Died of the Chroop aged 2 years and 11 months [see above, 21 April]
18 a Child Burned at Gleaston about 3 years Old burned so badly by its Close taking fire that it died in a few hours afterwards
26 John Gardner of Dalton Died aged 63 years

June

20 Smith Groom to Mr Michaelson of Barrow Isle Married to Margt Harrinson daughter of E. Harrinson Innkeeper Barrow
King William IV died aged 71 years
23 laid our Horses out

July

8 Thos Bows sheep shearing Henry and myself went and found all well
begun to Cut our Seed Grass July 1 Do our Meddow Grass 8 July

Aug

20 4 young Cattle Killd by the thunder at Stewner near Dalton
21 begun to shear Shore out 8 Septr got all our White grain 22 Septr Shore out Beans 26 Septr Octr 9 had done Housing Beans
23 Jane Dixon married to Thos Ainsworth at Walney Chaple

Septr

1 Richd Nichaleson Married to Hannah Cooper of Scals [Scales]
17 Elsey King died aged 52 years

Octr

4 begun to sow Wheat had done on the 6 a verry fine season
21 Laid our cows in 29 laid our horses in
28 John Threlfa Married to Mary Twonson [?] of Woodgate nr Ulverston||

Novr

14 Joseph Fisher Married to Ann Storey of Rampside
Robt Geldart of Hull Married to Ann Jackson of Leece 5th Novr 1837
Agness Lowise of Beck-side nr Urswick Died 4 Novr 1837
Mrs Susannah Simpson of Leece Died 5 Novr 1837

Decr

12 begun to Plow
John Fisher Son of Joseph Fisher of Barrow died aged 12 years and 11 months his Death was ocashend by a fall into avessels hold about 17 days before

1838

March

14 Peggy alis Margret Dixon died very suddenly aged 66 years
30 begin to sow Beans April 9 begun to sow Oats 17 had done

April

Thos Fresh of Newbarns died aged [?] years
21 Wm Jas Fisher sailed in the steamer to Liverpool

May

1 Wm Jas Fisher went by the railway from L-pool to Walsal
11 Had done sowing Barly 15 had done setting potatos
22 Martha Butcher of Cockin [Cocken] Died after a lingering Illness aged 83 years
23 Elizabeth Gibson of Northscale Island of Walney Died aged 53 years

June

2 Betsy Garnett of Ulverston married to Mr Walsh of Backbarrow
Mathew Dixon married

May

26 two men named Anthony Hall and David Parkinson was suffocated at Stainton Iorn ore works by the cabbin taking fire and the smook decending down the shaft Hall has left a widow and seven Childer Parkinson has left a widow but no family
19 a man found on the shore near Rampside Suposed to one of the name of Falshaw who was drowned on the Ulverston Sands when asssting to get an Anker
A boy of the name of Thompson from Dalton was drowned whilst bathing on Ulverston sands
28 Queen Victore Crowned with great rejocying

July

7 Thos Bows sheep shearing I did not attend it being a wet day||

20 man belonging to the May Flower Captn Holliday was Drowned at Peil by the upsetting of the Boat

Aug

3 a man belonging to a fishing boat drowned by the upsetting of a boat near Peil [of] fouldry he was cast up on Roose Coat March 10 days after

Died on the 23 July Bridget Wife of George Hind Tailor Cheapside Lancaster aged 66 years

Died on the 1 August John Gibson of Northscale Island of Walney after a long sickness which he bore with Christian fortitude aged 25

3 Mrs Case of leece Died aged 78 years

19 James Wright wife of Plumpton Cottage Died aged 28 years

27 begun to shear Shore out 28 Sepr Shore out beans 5 Octr had Housed all our Wt Grain 10 Octr got our Beans Octr 12

Died on the 29 Septr Mr James Bolton yeoman Old Park near Ulverston aged 74 years

Septr

25 Ann Shearwin of Barrow Died aged 34 years

Octr

17 Begun to Sow Wheat had done 20 a verry fine seed time

Novr

18 Andrew Atkinson Died aged 58 years

Decr

9 Begun to plow

1839

Jany

3 a man fell from the topsail yard of larg brig laying in Piel Channel on the deck and was Killed

3 Isabella Brockbank of Salthous Died aged 91 years

7 a sevear Storm such as has not been for many years it partly unroofed maney houses and blew down many Stacks of grain and hay down we had 2 stacks of hay blown down and a deal of it carried away with the wind there was a great loss amongst the Shipping and many lives lost 4 or 5 vessels driven from there moring at Pile [of] Fouldrey and went a Shore of fouley [Foulney] Island but no lives lost||

15 Thos Fisher of Dalton died aged 75 years
20 a brig belonging to Wthaven with 300 ton of cols on bord was wrecked on the Moat Bank[34] the hands were all saved

April

22 Begin to sow beans and Oats on the 3 had done on the 10th
25 Begun to sow Barly had done May 6 had done setting potatos May 8
29 John Wright of Plunton Cottage put an end to his existance by Hanging himself aged 60

May

9 Henry Danson of Dalton Died of a consumtion aged 22 years
25 Wm Harrinson son of Wm & Elizth Harrinson died aged 7 Months

June

4 John Patterson of Holebeck Married to Margret Brockbank Daughter of Thos Brockbank of Salthouse
14 Mrs Patterson Mother to the above John Patterson Died very Suddenly She was found dead in Bed had no previous Sickness
15 Christopher Ashburner Married to Betty Heslam
29 Ellener Cockerton Married to Wm Cragg of Ronehead
Begun to cut our seedgrass on the 24 June Do our Meddows July 7

July

6 Thos Bows Sheep shearing
3 Ann Park Died aged about 32 years
6 Mr John Bell of Kendal Died aged 70 years
20 Thos Hunter of Sourby Hall Married to Agness Kendal of Salthouse

Augt

22 Begun to shear had done Shearing white Grain 21 Septr Do beans 4 Octr

Octr

4 had housed all our Wt grain after avery tedious season

Septr

11 Samuel Redhead of Northscale Isle of Walney died many years a respectable farmer at that place aged 62 years
29 the Revr John Troughton died aged 64 years Minister of the Isle of Walney||
21 Begun to sow Wheat had done 29
31 had done getting Potatos

Dec

2 John Harrinson Died aged 39 years
4 Thos Park Died aged 38 years
9 begun to plow

20 John Davidson and John Diamond wear found Dead in a lime kiln belonging to Mr Richd Park, Sandwell near Ulverston the had gone in there to take there frugal meal it is suposed that a rush of gas had occurred which had cosed instant death as one of them had apiece of bred in his hand

20 the Brigantine Tejo, of Lisbon, F Moria de Olivernia, from Lisbon to Liverpool laden with woll was wrecked off Walney Island the crew and cargo saved the crew are all Portuguese the vessel broke up a few days afterwards

1840

Jany

17 Elizabeth Presow Daughter of Joseph Fisher of Barrow Died after a long sickness aged 33 years

20 Thos Patterson of Holebeck Died aged 24 years

Febry

4 Thos Thexton son of Robt and Margt Thexton died aged 22 months

14 Mrs Strich of the Island of Walney died in Child Bed aged 28 years||

5 Benjamin Kirkby of Ulverston Shoe Maker with his Son and Daughter and Mrs Parker there loger went on an Excursion to the Chaple Island and wandred down to a place called elwood Scare and was surrounded by the tide and in attempting to wade through his son and Daughter with Mrs Parker wear Drowned but he suceed in getting on to Chaple Island where he was taken of by a person in a boat Mrs Parker and his Daughter was found near the place after the tide returned but his son has not been found at the time I wright this Feby 23

21 John Bows of Lady Hall in thwaits Cumberland Died aged 64 years he was found dead in Bed

25 Thos King Married to Betty Walker of Kirkby

25 Capt Cannon vessel Launched[35]

March

5 James Simpson Died aged 83 years

5 as William Thompson and James Kendal of Martin were sitting upon a plank at Lindal Iorn Ore works the ground fell in and buried them about 3 yards deep the were dug out immedatly but quite dead several others wear upon the Same place but all escaped unhurt Thompson was upwards of 70 years old and Kendal about 52 years

9 William Sherwin of Barrow died aged 76 years

17 Begun to Sow Beans 18 sowed some Pees and 3 rigs of Oats through wating a very fine season the land in exelent Order

21 Ellinour Cornthwaite Daughter of Ellen and Richd Cornthwaite died aged 13 Months

28 had done sowing Oats

28 James Ray died aged 85 years||

April

16 Begun to set potatos had done 18
22 Begun to sow Barley had don 1st May a very dry season

May

29 Laid our Cows out

June

4 Laid our Horses out
29 Begun to cut our Seed Grass

July

4 Thos Bows Sheep shearing did not attend it being stormy
10 Begun to Cut our Medow Grass
18 Ann Simpson died aged 68

Aug

18 Begun to Shear Shore out 10 Sept Do Beans 22nd Sept

Septr

30 had Housed all our White grain Octr 6 had housed allour Beans

Oct

8 Begun to sow Wheat had done on the 15 after avery fine season
23 laid our Milk Cow in

Decr

12 John Winder Married to Margaret Horn at Wthaven
26 Philip Hartley Fisher of Barrow Married at Aldingham to Rebecca Diamond of Roosebeck same day John Atkinson of Barrow Married Isabella Brunt of Dalton same day Thos Barrow of Rosside Married to Mary Hudson of Ulverston

1841

January

25 Miles and Joseph Turner came to our House and the next Morning Miles went to survey Mr Langs estate in Walney and left here on the 28th

Feby

1 Robt Pattersons boon plough[36] at Barrow with 62 ploughs same Day the Harbour Master entered upon his situation at Barrow also same Day the Wet [Thwaite] Flat Iron Ore was first led to Barrow

On the 24th Jany two young men of the name of Robinson and Ormandy of Ulverston had been to Invite some of there Friends in Cartmel to the Odd Fellows ball at the Kings Arms Inn in Ulverston and on there return home in the evening the wear lost upon the sand and when found next morning the horse and gig was stuck fast in the channel and one of the men entangled aboute the step of the gig the other was found a little below in some fishing nets the wear a long way below the foard||

8 Richard Jackson of Roose Died aged 83 years much respected by all who knew him

24 George Cockerton of Dalton Died aged 78 years

April

3 Thos Bolton of Stank put an end to his existance by Hanging himself in a pig stey aged 70 years

13 Thos Thompson of Dalton Died aged 97 years

19 James Blendal was diking near the Wind Mill in the Island of Walney when an Iron bar between 3 and 4 foot long which was attached to the arm came off and struck him (who was 300 yards from the place) below the Shoulder blade and nearly severed his arm from his body Leveing it dangling by his side hanging only by a piece of skin and breaking several of his ribs the arm was [amputated] just below the Shoulder joint but he only survived eight or ten days when Death put an end to his Sufferings

May

2 Died at Old Park near Dalton in Furness Mr John Heslam late of the Island of Walney aged 81 years his Wife who is living is about the same age and his Wifes Mother who lives in the same house is just in her 100 year

6 Mathew Dixon Died aged 64 years[37]

12 Begun to sow Barley had don 15 a verry wet season

21 Begun to set potatos had done [?]

20 Henry Qualey Died aged 71 years

25 Miss Atkinson of Dalton Married to Mr Bolden of Lancaster

31 Thos Heslam of Barrow married to [blank] Lowrey of ramside

July

3 Henery and I went to Thos Bows Sheep Shearing and returned on the 5 had a verry Stormy jorney home

5 Joseph Jackson of Leece died after along Indisposion which he bore with Cristian fortitude aged 60 years||

August

23 Cathrine Dixon from Scotland Died aged 63 years

23 begun to Shear Septr 22 Shore all our Wt grain 24 shore out Beans

Octr

9 Wm Butler of Dalton Married to Mary Hartley Daughter of Mr Philip Hartley of Ulverstone

11 John Hartley of Sinkfall near Dalton Married to Ellen Atkinson Daughter of Wm Atkinson of Lindle

18 Thos Phizakley died at Salthous aged 74 years

11 Thos Lowrey of Dalton Killd at Butsbeck Iorn Ore works by aporishon of the roof comming down upon him tow or three more had a narrow escap it was two days and a night before the got him out

15 George Huddelston Married to Mary Milburn of Newbarns
Wm Lowry Married to Agness Fisher of Barrow
Wm King Married to Ellen Lowery of Ramside

17 Wm Slater of Park married to Sarah Case of Manner Abby [Manor Abbey] all the above at Dalton Church

Nov

29 Joseph Winder of Beclif [Baycliff] Married to Ellen Jackson of Ramside

Dec

2 Married at St Mary's church Lancaster by the Rev Robert Gibson, vicar of Bolton le Sands Thomas Yeats Parker Michaelson Esqr.[38] of the Isle of Barrow to Jane eldest Daughter of the late Charles Gibson Esqr of Quernmore Park in this County||

1842

January

4 Lenard Addinson of roosebeck Died aged 77 years

6 a son of Joseph Ormandy of Lindal Black smith was drowned Whilst Scating on the Ice near Lindle Coat aged about 10 years of Age

15* Margt Butcher of Old Park formerly of the Island of Walney Died at the great age of 98 years

*the above Margt Butcher was 15 years blind but all her Other faculties good to the last she was the Mother of 10 Children grandmother to 53 and great grandmother to 127 and great great grandmother to 16

14 Ellen Waters of Northscale in the Island of Walney Died aged 80 years

25 Prince of Wales christening

Do an unfortunate accident occurred at Conishead Priory at the rejoicing of the Prince of Wales christining as a man of the name of Thomas Jackson nursery gardener at the Priory, was engaged about loading a cannon in front of the house, it accidentally went off and blew off both the poor fellows arms. He lingered a few hours and then expired.

Feby

22 Betty Creary wife of Richd Creary red Lion Dalton died aged 46 years

March

11 Abraham Slater of Dalton Died aged 77 years

April

4 begun to Sow Oats
4 Nathan Dickinson married to Cathran Hodgson the bridegroom aged 19 & the bride not Quite 14 years||
23 finished sowing our fallow Oats
26 finished Setting potatos

May

4 had done sowing Barley a fine dry season
6 son John went to L Pool entred on his situation at Mr Carters Drugist
13 Betty Simpson of Leece Died aged 77

July

2 Henry and I went to Thos Bows Sheep Shering returned on the 5 the 4 being a verry wet and stormy day
12 Mary Bolton of North Scale Island of Walney Died aged 88 years

Augt

9 Begun to Shear Shore out 7 Septr do Beans 8

Septr

16 had secured all our Wt gran Do 19 had housed all our Beans
Died at Piel Island Joseph Gould on the first september aged 62 years
Jane Lowther Married to Christopher Thornborrow on the 3 Septr.
married on 14 Septr H. W. Schneider esq.,[39] of Southgate Middlesex to Augusta second Daughter of Richd Smith of Bank field near Urswick died also on the 14 at Leece in Low Furness Mr Wm Bryers yeoman in the 90 years of his age
20 Miss Betsy Busher dress maker Died at Kendal aged 65 years
22 William Robinson[40] of Barrow met with a fatle accident in comming from Ulverstone Market on getting on to the cart head in Dalton went his foot shipped and having a young horse it became unruly and he was thrown down under the wheels and had his head sadly brused and cut as well as other parts of his body he lingred in great pain till the following afternoon when death put an end to his sufferings aged 37 years

Octr

5 had done gitting potatos a verry dry season and good crop||

Novr

6 John Jackson above gate Leece Died aged [blank] years
11 Mr William Seatle Grocer of Ulverston Died with only a few Hours Sickness aged 52 years
14 Henery Grimes Married to Betty Hullock at Dalton Church

1843

Jany

2 Thos Sherwin Married to Mary Dixon at Dalton
7 John Falshaw Married to Bellow Atkinson at Dalton Church
10 Thos Jackson of Millom Cumberland Married to Elizabeth Walton of Barrow
11 Fanny Robinson Died aged 62 years
on the 24 Feby after a short illiness at Duddon Grove near Broughton in Furness in his 67 year the Revd Wm Millais BD formerly fellow and tutor of St. Johns Cambridge

March

22 begun to sow Beans 25 begun to sow Oats
a Mellancolly accident happned to Wm son of Walter Comber he was going out with his gun to shoot Daukers [Furness dialect: ducks] he unfortunatly in going over a stile and the peice went off and they contents loged in both his thigs this was about 11 oclock in the morning and he died about 6 the same Evening aged 22 years

April

20 Robert Brocklebunt Married to Mary Lesh Daughter of Edward Lesh both of newbarns||

July

1 Richd Went to Thos Bows Sheep Shearing and returned on 3rd the 2nd Being wet and stormy found Thos only very poorley
28 at the Isle of Barrow the Lady of T. Y. P. Michaelson of a son and air
31 the Fanney of fleetwood Captr Rimmer sunk in Pile Channel and two men Drowned Viz James Scot Sailor 38 years a single man and Wm Garth 27 years Labourer has left a Wife and 3 Childer the Captn saved himself by getting into the riggin and was taken off by some Fisher men and landed at Piel Island Scot was found by James Hool near the low point of Barrow Isle and was brought to Barrow Garth was found on the back side of Walney Isle near South end on the 11 August and also Brought to Barrow a Corrners Inquest was held the Virdits in both Cases Accindatel the both belonged to Ulverstone[41]
31 Died at the Isle of Barrow the infant son of T. Y. P. Michalson esq.
27 Jane Gibson Married to Richd Hunter of Scales park
31 Ellin Storey Wife of Captn James Story of the Victoria Died at Liverpool aged 53 years

Augt

21 begun to Shear Shore out our White grain 13 Septr had Housed all our Wt Grain 23 Septr had shore all our Beans Septr 21

Septr

11 Mary Postlethwaite Wife of Wm Postlethwaite of Barrow Isle was found Dead in the Stares it was suposed that she had got up to see the Clock and had falen down in a fit aged 63 years||

24 Captn James Cannon Died at Ulverston aged 66 years

Octr

2 Elizabeth Second Daughter of Capn James Barrow died after a long illness which she bore with Christian fortidue and resignation aged 30 years

Novr

12 Thos Wignal Wife of Dalton was Burned to Death by her Close taking fire when in a state of Drunkness

25 John Jackson of Leece Married to Eliza Nelson of Pennybridge

29 Died Joseph Yarker Esqr Dykelands Collector of the Customs Ulverston aged 84 years

Decr

5 Mary Kendal was floating in Duddon and was taken out of the water by some Sailors quite Dead it was suposed she had drowned herself a very short time before aged about 19 years

1844

Jany

19 John Rawlinson of Ramside left a Neighbours House to go to his own and has not since been Heard off now 4th Feby

18 a young Woman Poisned her self by taking arsnick Suposed to a disapointment in a Love afair

17 Thos Bows of Fennwick died after a long illness aged 69 years Jany 17 3 oclock in the morning

Feby

1 John Hartley Seiner [Senior?] of Sinkfall was drowned in attempting to Cross the Duddon Sands on foot he only Left home about noon and was brought back the same evening a Corps||

4 The new Chapel at three lanes end Barrow was Opened by they Reverend John Boldwin [Baldwin] Dalton the congregation was so large that maney wear Obliged to stand at the outside[42]

March

12 John the son of Mr Thomas Butler of Dalton Died of Consumption Aged 20 years

April

8 Begun to Sow Oats

June

24 Begun to Cut our Seed Grass

August

13 Jame Thornburrow daughter of Christ & Margt Lowther of Rooscoat died after a long illness aged [?]
13 begun to Shear Shore out on 28 Septr
30 begun to sow Wheat had done 3 October
My son John Fisher saild from Liverpool on the 13 Augt 1844 in the ship St George Capt Ferris burdin 900 tons he with 11 others Cabin Passengers and 200 Do in the second Cabin and Stearage and arrived in New York in 31 days after a fine Passage left New York on the 15 Septr and Travled by Steam Boat Railway and Stage Coach to Browns Vill [Brownsville, Pennsylvania] a distance of about 300 miles in 50 Hours and found his Uncle and other Friends well[43]

Septr

26 My niece Agness Fisher in Company with 2 Miss Lethams and Mrs Cadet a west Indian came to see us
Richd Fisher Married to Elzabeth Denny of Lindal Oct 12[44]

1845

Feby

6 Robt Greenwood of Northskale Island of Walney Died aged 85 years
15 Died Jane the last surviving Daughter of Thomas Butler esq., conveyancer aged 17 years

March

27 James Cock[45] came to Barrow and left again on the 31 he had been 15 years up the Meditrainna [Mediterranean]

April

2 Married Thomas Roper of Liverpool to Elizabeth Case Eldest Daughter of Robt. Case of Ulverston tinman and Brazier||
2 begun to sow Beans Do Oats April 3
Married on the 31 March John Case of Roosebeck to Miss Bolton of Ulverston Daughter of the late Wm Bolton of Park House
25 had done sowing Barley the Land in good order

May

17 a Coronor Inquest was held on the body of Rob Winter aged about 30 years a native of Lowther in Westmorland who was drowned whilst baithing at Barrow he was a work man at the rail way[46]

July

5 Thos Bows Sheep Shearing[47]

Augt

20 begun to Shear Septr 13 Shore out White grain verry fine weather for 3 week only lost $\frac{1}{4}$ of a day

Septr

23 Died Mary Elizabeth Dauckter of James Tyson Inkeeper Barrow aged 11 Months

Octr

16 William Bows of Fenwick died of the Bloddy flux was only Poorly about three weeks aged 26 years

21 we housed our Beans a verry heavy Crop in the far Moor

22 begun to Sow Wheat 24 had sown all our Summer fallow

Novr

14 Died at Ulverston in child-bed aged 33 years Martha the truly amiable and beloved wife of John Denny druggist

14 Mrs Walker of North Scale Ile of Walney Died advanced in years||

20 Wm Danson the last surviving son of Sarah Danson of Dalton died aged 25 years

Died at Ulverston on Friday the 14 Novr in childbed aged 33 years Martha the truly amiable and beloved wife of Mr John Denny druggist [Repeated entry]

Died at Northscale Isle of Walney on the 14 Novr Mrs Walker advanced in years

27 Richd Robinson Butcher of lane Hous near Ulverstone put an end to his Life by handing himself a corner [coroner] Jurey sat upon the Body Virdit Temperry Insanaty

Died in Octr a child of James Tysons Barrow aged about 11 months

1846

March

1 Died at Barrow M. Daker aged 82 years

Railway on the 30th April the locomotive engin belonging to the Furness Railway was for the first time driven up to Kirkby Ireleth. After staying for some time she departed for Barrow[48]

May

10 Henry Houghton a youth 16 years of age unfortunately fell under one of the Waggons of the furness Railway and had his legs so much crushed that he died a few days after of inflamation

a mellancoly los of life 9 Persons in attempting to Cros the Sands from Ulverstone to Cartmell on the 4 May got into what the call Black scare hole which is a hole 13 feet deep at Low Water the wear all in one Cart every one with the horse Perrished it was suposed that the weare the wors for licquor

June

5 Wm Sherwin Died after along Illiness aged about 15 years

15 Richardson Gibson Married to Sarah Kellet both of Hawcoat Near Dalton

16 James Mason Draper Married to Mary Fell Daughter of George Fell of Sunderland terris Ulverstone||

July

16 Wm Wilson a labourer on Furness railway 22 years of age who through inadvertance had placed Himself betwixt two Waggons one of which moving when his knee was caught betwixt them which cosed acompound fracture ending in mortification and Died 7 days after

26 Margt Bows of Fenwick Died aged 68 years

Augt

4 begun to Shear Shore all our Wt grain 10 Septr Beans 12 Do

Elizabeth Daughter of James & Mary Bolton[49] Born on the 18 Feby 1841 Died August 18 1846 aged 5 years on the 15 Augt Thos Powlesland Custom Hous Officer his son a youth about 16 years of age and George Marton a Custom House Officer was Drowned near Conckle Pier [near Rampside] suposed by the upsetting of there boat

24 the Railway from Roa to Dalton opened for Passanger[50]

5 James Cock[51] was discharged from the 5th Regt Fusiliers, in Ireland, Came to see us on the 17th and sailed on the 25th in the packet ship Niagara for New York N.A.

Septr

4 Richard Coward of Little Mill Died aged 46 years

17 Mrs Margt Hartley widdow of late John Hartley of Dalton died aged 79 years

30 Martin Coward Died aged 19 years

October

12 Robt Dixon Died aged 40 years

5 begun to sow Wt [Wheat] had done on the 7 a very fine Season came on rain the next day and continued for above a week after||

Married at Dalton on the 22 Septr George Patterson of Holbeck to Mary Ann youngest daughter of Thos Brockbank of Salthouse both in Low Furness

7 Henry Patterson of Hollbeck married to [blank] Gradwell
14 Married John Ashburner of Beckside Dalton to Miss Colton Daughter of George Coulton Dendron
24 Ellen Jackson of Roose Died aged 85 years much respected

1847

Jany

16 William Atkinson of Lindal Died aged 60 years
19 Betty Simpson of Barrow Died aged 86 years[52]
24 Elizabeth Gibson wife of Thos Gibson of Hawcoat died aged . . . years
28 Anty Garnett Son of John Barker Grocer Market Street Ulverston died aged 4 months

Feby

1 John Barker died at Hill Top Sawrey near Hawkshead aged 79 years

March

15 Begun to Sow Beans
16 Begun to Sow Oats had done on the 24 a very nice Seed time and the Land in fine order
Margt Coupland of Broughton Died aged 66 years on the 13 March
18 George Kendal of Salthous Died aged 75 years
21 Frances Widders of Southend Isle of Walney Died aged 89 years

April

6 Mr James Walls of Hawkshead Married to Miss Phassacklea of Salthous Low Furness
6 Died at Rampside Low Furness Henery Lowrey aged 88 years
Died at Barrow on the 1 instand Philip Gand son of John Hartley aged 8 months||
19 Begin to sow Barley had done May 1
Potatos Sold in Ulverstone Market at 2/2 p stone and Eggs at 2d per Egg
had finished setting potatos May 7th
27 Henry Robinson Chemist Married to Jane Penny both of Ulverstone April 27
30 Died at Ulverston Margret Wild third Daughter of Mr Samuel Tyson Attorney aged 23 years much respected

May

7 Died very suddenly Mr Thos Rigg late collector of the Customs Ulverstone aged 71 years much respected
12 James Hartley Married to Elizabeth Pecthall of Holm Bank [near Great Urswick]

June

10 Wm. Simpson of Southend Island of Walney Died aged 60 years
5 Died at Rakesmoor near Dalton Miles Shaw in the 72 year of his age
19 Plato Buttler son Mr Buttler Dalton Died aged 21 year after a protracted illness which he with Christian resignation and exemplary fortitude

July

8 Died Wm Son of Thomas Bolton of Ramside aged 32 years

Augt

1 Mary wife of Thos Greenwood Died aged [?]
2 Thomas Show married to Ann Rumney
9 Begun to Shear had shore all our White grain Augt 31st

Septr

4 had done Shearing Beans
2 Robert Jackson a Clerk at the Railway Peer Died age [?]
16 Sept Died at Newbarns Margt Fresh aged about 70 years
24 Capt Wm Janes of the Sconer Mounten Maide of Cardif in going on borde fell from a plank and was killd on the spot||

Oct

1 begun to sow Wheat and had done on the 4 Octr with fine Season
George Hind of Lancaster Died Septr 24 aged 85 years
2 A labouring man of the name of Wm Johnson was Stabbed at Dalton in Furness by a person named Myers also a labourer it appears Johnson was proceding home about twelve oclock at night he was overtaken by Myers a quarrel encued when Myers drew a Knife and Stabbed him in several parts of his body he now lies in a dangerous State one of his arms which was severely alcerated [lacerated] and some of the arteries divided has been amputated Myers is in custody the knife which he used was found in a garden near to his lodgings he was taken in bed soon after—Johnson Died on they 15th same Month[53]
5 Died in Market Street Lancaster Jane Wife of Richd Wearing aged 39 years
7 Died at Biggar in Walney Agness daughter of Thos J. Woodurn aged 23 years

Nov

18 Killed on the Dalton Railway a man named Spencer by 3 wagons running over him breaking both his thighs he died about 2 hours after
20 Married at Dalton by the Revd Mr Morgan Curate Mr Leonard Gould of North Scale, to Miss Simpson of Southend same time and place Mr Jno Jackson of Biggar to Miss Gould of Northscale all in Isle of Walney same time and place Mr Jno Gawith tailor & Draper of Rosecote to Miss Woodburn of Biggar Isle of Walney same time and place Mr Charles Allen to Miss Mary Slater both of Hawcoat and also at the same time and place Mr Joseph Uren of Stank to Miss Tomlinson of Hawcoat||
8 Drowned on Duddon Sands Mr Wm Postlethwaite of Beckside Kirkby Ireleth he had only been gone from home about $\frac{1}{2}$ an hour when the horse returned without him and the Saddle under its Belly

1848

January

8 at Whastings [Hastings] Sussex on the 8 Instant to which plase she had resorted for the benfit of her health Elizabeth Wife of the Revd J. Baldwin A.M. Dalton-in-Furness in the 44 year of her age in this Lady the poor of Dalton have lost a most inestimable friend
20 James Kirkby of Hawcoat died aged 51
27 John Kinish back smith and Farmer at Northsale Isle of Walney was Comming from the Market and set to cross [the ford] before it was tide he had a Horse and Cart with two young Piggs in it the wear all Drowned he had pertaken rather too freely of John barly corn the wear all found the next morning not fare off he was 45 years of age

February

9 the Smak Friends of new Quay Captn Davis Corn laden was driven on shore on the back of Walney Isle some of the corn was washed out and the remainder was discharged and sold to Robt Benson of Northend Mill the vessel is though [thought] will be got off again

March

5 the Revd William Slater of Northscale Island of Walney was drowned in comming from the Marriage of T. J. Woodburns Daughter of Bigger he had got out of the rode [i.e. the ford] and was mired and could not Extracate himself

April

1 begun to sow Beans 3d Oats had done on the 6 only a verry wet season||
21 James Fell Died at Fleetwood but late of the Island Walney aged 75 years he was Intered at Dalton in Furnas on the 24
29 James Troughton of Liverpool Married to Miss Crag of Biggar in the island of Walney the wear Married at Walney Chaple by the Revd J. Park
25 Thos Woodburn of Ulverston Solisitor Married to Mary Ann Park of Lancaster daughter of the late Thomas Park

May

2 had done setting Potatos 3 begun to sow barley Finished sowing on the 9 May
Died at Dalton on the May Elizabeth Ann Daughter of Wm Butler in the 5th year of her age
5 Died at Newbarns in Low Furness Mrs Lish in the 55 year of her age
21 George Slater of Dalton but late of Park Farm Near Dalton died aged 73 years
26 Died at Irleth Miss Towers advanced in years

June

6 Abraham Fisher of Dalton died aged 47
Mary Walton of Barrow married to [blank] on the 28 May

July

8 William Bolton of Northscale Isle of Walney died aged 94 years
9 Rachael Robinson Married to John Eden Black Smith at Barrow [Railway] Station
19 had got all our meddow hay a verry fine season||

Augt

5 William Fell droped down Dead whilst helping to discharge ballast at Barrow Pear aged 34 years
7 begun to Shear Wheat had done shearing our White grain on Septr 12 on 16 Beans

Septr

26 begun to sow Wt had done the 30 a verry fine season and the land in Exelent order

Novr

11 Two boys Henry James Riley Children of John Riley a labouring man of Dalton the wear surended by the tide on Duddon sand whilst gathering Cockls the younger about 11 years old lost his life
13 a Daughter of Robert Davis carpinter of Newbarns was burned to death by her Close taking fire whilst placing a pan on the fire she was 8 years of age
25 a boy lost his life at Orgrave Mill Iorn works [near Dalton] by his close getting entangled in the Masenery he was drown in and Kild Instantainsly aged 15 years
Died at Ulverston Allan Backhous corn dealer and formerly of Newby aged 79 years Novr 14 1848
Agness daughter of Wm and Elizabeth Denny of Lindal Died of Typhus Fever aged 13 years 24 Novr 1848

Decr

4 A man drowned at Barrow Richd Acton of the flat Waterloo of Chester was drowned while attempting to get on board his vessel at Barrow Pier the night being verry dark he was found about 4 hours after aged 35 years
29 Died the Revd Joseph Thomson Kirkbank 25 years Vicker of Dalton much respected aged 54 years||

1849

Jany

9 Died at Barrow at the House of her son Mrs Ann Holm late of Kirkby in the 92nd year of her age

Feby

26 Died at Leece James Jackson aged 79 years

March

4 Mr Morgan entered on his duties as Vicar of Dalton and read the Thirty Nine Articles of Religion

20 Sowed our Beans 21 begun to sow Oats had done sowing Oats the 28 the land in verry nice Order

April

24 had done setting Potatos

26 Begun to sow Barley had done May 2nd

21 the Reverd Dr Stonard of Aldingham Died aged 81 years

May

1 Died the beloved wife of Robert Town Esqr at Brown How aged 31 years

7 a sailor fell from the top mast of the Brig Maria then laying at Barrow and piched on the rail of the vessel and then on to the sand and was killd on the spot he has left a Wife and one Child to lament his loss he was about 27 years of age

12 Fatal accident at Barrow by the upsetting of a Boat by which three men was Drowned Viz George Dixon aged 29 years Thos Jackson aged 25 and David King son of Thos King farmer at Barrow aged 20 years

June

15 begun to cut our seed Grass had got all our Medow hay 16 July

25 Abraham Atkinson of Dalton Died after about a quarter of an hours illness aged 45 years

July

3 George Bolton of Rampsid Married to Mary eldest Daughter of Thos Coward of Colt Park the wear Married at Sent Silas's Church Liverpool||

Augt

20 George Gibson of Northscales Island of Walney Died in the 67 year of his age

20 John McKay Tea dealer and Traveler from Preston died verry suddenly at Hawcoat Begun to shere on the 6 August had done Shearing 7 Sepr our White grain and on the 10 our beans had housed all our White grain on September 14 Beans on 22

Septr

24 begun to sow Wheat a very nice season

24 Thos King junr Married to Elizabeth Brocklebank of Kirkby

Octr

6 William Greenwood Northscale Island of Walney Died aged 64 years

Novr

15 James Creary of Dalton Died aged 48
18 Elizabeth Kendal wife of James Kendal of Salthouse Died in Childbed aged 36 years
30 James Hartley Wife of Pennington Died in child bed aged 34 years

Decr

1 Elizabeth Relect of the late John Gardner of the White horse Inn Dalton Died aged 71 years
5 the Revd James Morrison Morgan Vicar of Dalton Married to the Widow of the Revd William Spence late of Dalton
8 Thos Bell cordwaner Barrow Married to [blank] Spence daughter of Richd Spence farmer Bigger in the Island of Walney
3 Birth at the Isle of Barrow the Lady of T.Y.P. Michaelson Esqr of a son||
11 Captn Parry of the slope St. George of Liverpool laying at Barrow Pear was drowned whilst endevering to get on Bord his Vessel he was 31 years of age
a young man of the name Dickinson in atempting to cross Kirkby More [Moor] on the 10 Decr the weather being wet and a thick mist set in is suposed he had lost his was [way] and fell into a slate quarry and was Kild on the Spot he was found when the workmen went to work the same morning he set out about 6 oclock was about 17 year Old

1850

Jany

17 Died Mary Elizabeth daughter of James and Mary Tyson Innkeeper Barrow aged 9 Months

Febry

10 Thos Hartley of Dalton Died aged 72 years Much respected

March

21 begun to sow Oats sowed two days came on weather that stoped us 3 weeks and 3 days finished on 18 April
31 James Brockbank an aprentes with Mr Hall surgon Dalton Died by taking Poison the jures Virdit Fello d see [Felo de se: suicide] he was burried at 10 oclock at night without burial service[55]

April

3 Isabella Hartley Daughter of John and Elizh Hartley of Barrow Died from Inflametion of Wind pipe aged 10 years
21 Elsabeth Deny of Lindal Died after along Sickness aged 57 years
30 James Robinson of Lane House near Ulverston married Miss Mary Fleming of Field Foot Ridal [Rydal]

May

1 Thomas son of William Kendal of Salthous married to Dorothy Second Daughter of Mr William Ormandy of Gleaston Castle||

12 Died at Backbarrow John Garnett late of Ulverston Much and deservedly respected by all who had the plasure of his acquentance aged 73 years

At Old-park near Ireleth on the 19 Sarah widdow of the late John Heslam of Biggar in the Island of Walney aged 85 years

June

2 Mary Creary of Dalton in her 83 year

18 Thos Colton of Dendron Married to Briget Slater Daughter of the late Geo Slater formerly of Park Farm near Dalton

23 begun to cut our seed Grass

July

25 Thos Dixon of Dalton met with his death under following Sircumstances he was carting Iorn ore from Eliscals to wate [Thwaite] Flat and in desinding the Steep hill at St. Hellins the stays of one of the horses broke and the animal took fright and diseased in is attemp to stop it was thrown backward on the rood and the Cart passed over him nearly severing his hed from his body and killing him instantly he was 51 years of age

Augt

12 begun to shear Shore out 9 Septr had housed all our grain 18 Septr

12 Thos Fisher Married to Miss Charnley of Pear Tree Kirkby Ireleth

23 Henry Hodgson Mate of the Alexander of Whitehaven was found dead in his birth virdict of the Jurey Died of apoplexy

23 James Harris a miner at Whitrigges Iorn Ore works was killed by a bucket faling down a shaft 50 yards deep and killing him on the spot

Septr

7 Thos Kendal Landlord of the Ship Inn Barrow Died 29 years

14 Thos Winder Married to Ruth Parkinson||

Octr

17 John Kay a ship carpinter was Shot Dead on the spot In an afray on Duddon sand by Samuel Todd a fisherman from Dalton commeted to Lancaster Castle for trial at the Assises and Transported beyond seas for the term of seven years

Novr

13 William Kendal of Salthouse Married to Sarah Hunter of Moss Side

16 James Kendal of Salthouse Married to Ann Swainson of Ulverston

18 Joseph Taylor Waller Married to Elizabeth Sherwen of Barrow

29 Died Jane Atkinson Wife of John Atkinson of Lindal aged 26 years

Decr

7 also died John Atkinson husband to the above aged 26 years
11 Died at Dalton Agnes Paxton aged 71 years she was interred at Walney Chaple
30 George Fell Died at Ulverston and Interd in the new churchyard there aged 67 years

1851

Feby

28 At the patten [Patent Ship Building] Slip Barrow Jane Daughter Edward Brockbank joiner aged 3 & on the 4 March Edward and John twin sons of the above aged 3 days[56]

March

6 Elizabeth Relict of the late Thos Harrinson innkeeper Barrow Died at Ulverston aged 73 years Interd at Dalton

April

4 begun to Sow Oats and finished the 9 a very nice season

May

28 Mr Wm. Turner came to see us and staid ouernight
29 Wm Denny junr of Lindal died aged 34 years

July

5 James Walton Married to [blank] Dixon daughter of late Isaac Dixon Tanner||

Augt

13 begun to Shear Shore out 10 Septr Shearers from 1/6 to 3/ per D.

Septr

27 had Howsed all our Grain
29 begun to Sow Wheat had Sown our summer fallow Oct 3
20 Died at Lyth near Kendal Miles Turner aged about 36 years much respected by all his Aquentance

Octr

7 Married the Revd J. Baldwin of Dalton to Mary Ann eldest daughter of John Bond Esqr of Lancaster
7 a son of John Dawsons a sailor was Drowned by falling out of a boat in Barrow Chanell
8 Died at Liverpool Mrs Betty Burns late of Whtaven in her 75th year
8 the great rusling mach [wrestling match] at Ulverston Jackson and Atkinson Suposed to be 7,000 Spectators present[57]

Novr

Wm Pool and Thos Lewis employed as Labours on the Furness Railway the wear crushed to Death by the Ingin and 12 wa[g]ons running over them

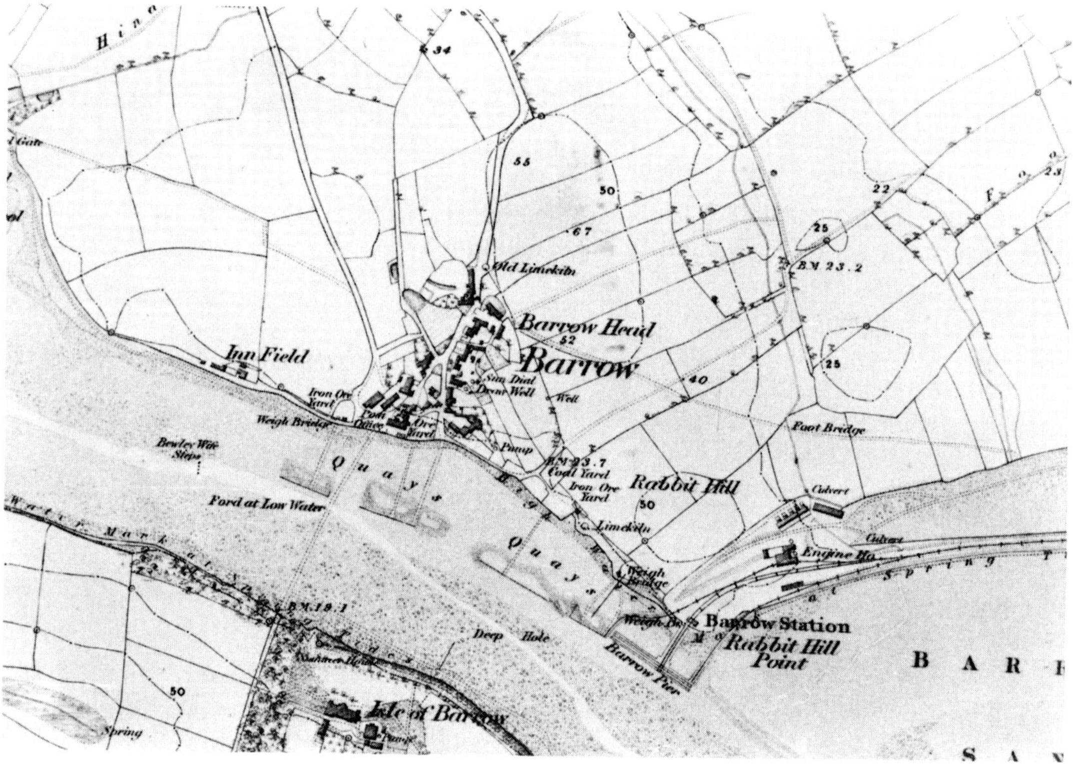

Fig. 5 Barrow Village, 1851. From the Ordnance Survey 6-inch map.

1852

Died at East Cottage Rampside on the 17 January awfully Suddon and deeply lamented Margt the beloved Wife of Mr George Case yeoman aged 61 years

March

15 Begun to sow Oats had done the 23

30 had set most part of our potatos in the field the land in verry good order we had a verry little rain from the Latter end of Feby till this time 29 had a good Shour

April

1 Considered to sow our potato and Turnip land with Oats Instead of Barley the weather being so fine||

July

29 begun to Shear had Shore out 26 Aug wages from 2/– 2/6 to 3/– per day

Septr

15 The first New Ship Built at Barrow 180 tons was Launched the day was beautiful all the Vessels had their Flags hoisted she was Christned by Mrs Roper Senr the Jane Roper in respect to Mrs Thos Roper of Newland House[58]

Octr

23 Samuel Smith was killd by faling out of a bucket in desinding an Iorn Pit at Park near Dalton

Novr

9 Agnes Fisher Liverpool and Agnes Clark Ulvr came to see us Thos Bowes came from Fenwick same day

12th Mr John Winder my WF Cousin died very suddenly with an attack of Paralissis the day

do following would have completed his 72 years of age

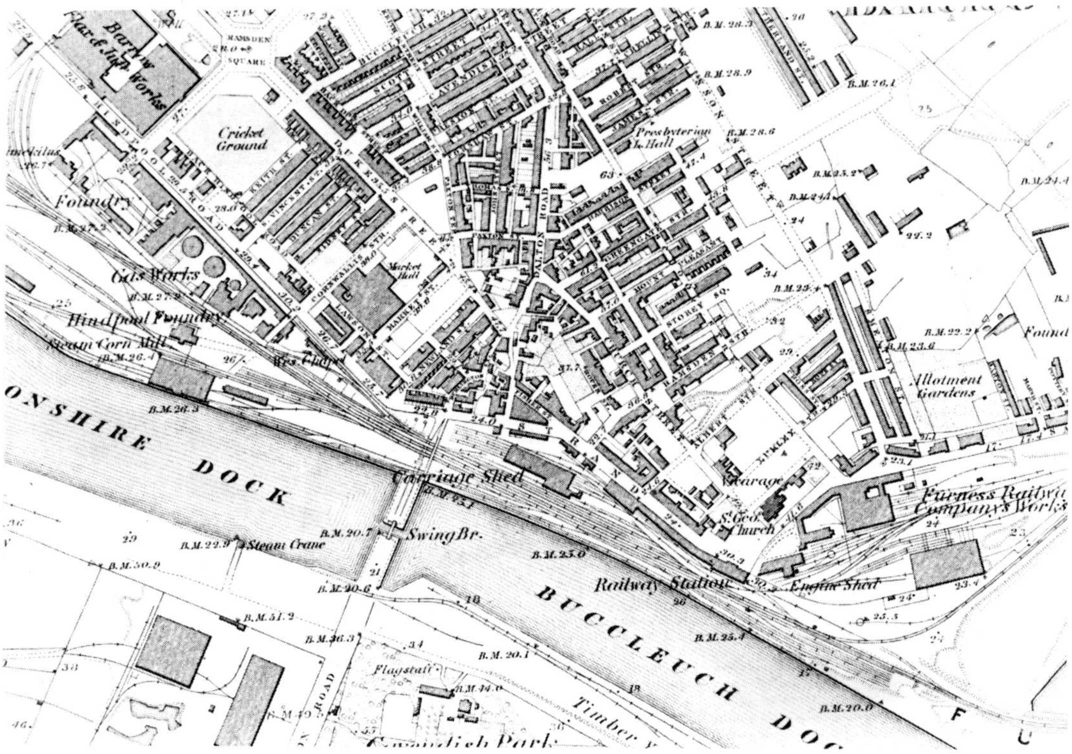

Fig. 6 Barrow, 1873. From the Ordnance Survey 6-inch map.

Decr

12 Mary[59] wife of James Bolton Inn Keeper Ulverston and Daughter of Wm Fisher Barrow Died awfully sudden aged 41 years, leaving six children (the infant 17 days old) to lament their sudden bereavement She was interd at the New Church Ulvn by the side of her little Daughter Elizabeth on the 15 Decr 1852. The baby Christned same day. Her brother Henry came from Wthaven to the funeral.

25 Christmas Day Morning a Storm commenced about between 2 & 3 Oclock & subsided about 8 or 9 in the forenoon was a Nice day had blown some Trees up in the Orchard and blown down Chimneys and Slates from Sundry Houses on the Morning of the 27 it came on again a perfect Hurricane doing great damage all over the Country||[60]

26 Son Henry left here for Wthaven Sunday Evening previous to the Storm, which washed down a deal of the embankment

12 Jane Wife of Robt. Brocklebank of Little Mill & Daughter of Edward Lesh of Newbarns Aged 32 years leaving 4 children the youngest a Month Old. [Entry out of sequence]

1853

Jany

4 The Revd W. L. Croft kindly adminsitered the Holy Sacrament to 7 aged persons who attended at Wm Fishers Viz William Fisher aged 77 John Fisher aged 75 Mrs Mary Ashburner aged 68 Margaret Fisher aged 68 years Mrs Gawith aged 76 years Jane Shaw aged 83 years Elizabeth Fell aged 76 years, sister to Mrs Shaw.

14 a little girl Daughter of Francis Trenouth Quarry Man was so dreadfully Burnt by her cloths taking fire in the absence of her mother that She only lived about 4 hours

19 John Ashburner Elliscales married to Mary Ann Daughter of the late Abraham Atkinson Auctioneer of Haume near Dalton

19 Died above Gate Leece Sarah Widow of the late John Jackson Yeoman aged 61 years her Sister-in-Law Miss Jane Jackson died a short time previous

23 Richard Fisher with his 2 Brothers in law went by Train to Wthaven[61] and to New Monkwray attended the Sale of John Briggs on the 24th and a sale near Harrington on the 25th returned home on the 26th||

21 Thos Bell a tenant in James's Terrace owned by Wm Fisher made an assignement

February

4 Alice Daughter of Joseph Fisher aged 3 years was on a visit to her Grandfathers Thos Storey late Officier of Customs and in play ran across the road Sunderland terrace Ulverston where she was knocked down by a cart laden with 26 cwt of Copper ore the wheel passed over her Boddy and killed her on the spot

7 At the Regester Office Ulverstone Mr William Walker Surveyor of the Furness Railway to Mary Annie Daughter of Mr Samuel Tyson attorney at Law all of Ulverstone

5 Mr John Denney Married to Betty Daughter of the late Richard Creary Inn Keeper all of Dalton

8 At St Brides Church Liverpool by the Revd W. Fallon the Revd W. Lewellyn Croft of Barrow in Furness Married to Maria Daughter of E Hinton Orme Esqr of Philadelphia

March

6 Christopher Ashburner Cordwainer and Inn Keeper Barrow Died aged 43 years

24 Died at Rampside aged 47 years Thomas Helme for upwards of 17 years the steady and faithful servant of the Revd W. Dawson of Rampside

30 Died at the residence of her Brother Mr Geo Case Rampside Agnes relict of the late Mr Layfield Cabinet Maker London aged 58 years

31 begun to sow Oats finished April 14

April

16 Married George Shaw to Mary Creary both of Barrow||

June

9 Married at Wallasy Church by the Revd W. Pollock M.A. of Liverpool James Ramsden[62] Esqr of Millwood to Annie Mary Daughter of Robert Edwards Esqr Liscard Cheshire.

Fig. 7 Barrow in 1870. By this time, the Fisher farm had been engulfed by a rash of red-brick buildings.

14 at the Cathedral Manchester by the Revd W. Wilson Roger Hesketh Barton Esqr Surgeon to Mary Anne second Daughter of George Hargraves Esqr Ulverstone.

July

18 as William Higgin and a Sailor aged 19 years was discharging Ballast from a Vessel they were both precipitated into the hold a depth of 14 feet Higgin badly hurt and the sailor Killed after the inquest next day he was interd at Dalton

13 William son of William Casson Shoe Maker died at Salthouse aged 13 weeks

Augt

14 Mrs Parker with her son and his Wife two Grandsons and a Grandaughter also Miss A Clark came from Ulverstone by Buss[63] and Rail to see us

17 begun To Shear Shore out 10 Septr
Sister Agnes & Isabella Story spent the day with us

20 son Henry came from Wthaven and returned on the 29 inst

Septr

13 James Bolton Ulverston Married to Margt Tyson Abbey Hotel[64]||

1854

Febry

8 five men blocked up in a Iorn Ore Pit at Park near Dalton by the bursting in of a pond of Water three was drowned and two taken out alive but one died the fowling [following] day

26 Revd William Lewellyn Croft preached his farewell sermon at Barrow[65] in the Evening to a deeply Affected and large congregation his Text 20 chap of Acts & part of 35th verse Remember the Words of the Lord Jesus—

March

2 A splended Bible a pocket comunion service & a handsome Surplice was present to him as a mark of the esteem in which he was held by his Congregational Members he was a Worthy Man and his Lady was as much respected for her kind visits in the Neighbourhood

5 Revd Thos Horsfall preached his first Sermon at Barrow

4 Mr John Case Tinman and Brazier married to Eliza Bell both of Ulverstone.

22 at Walton on the Hill Liverpool William K Chamney Married to Miss Ann Whineray Ulverston Milliner

April

5 Died at Hawcoat Agnes Wife of James Ecclesten on aged 61 years

10 Died at Broughton in Furness Miss Margaret Pritt aged 56 years

4 Died at Barrow Henry Gimries Labourer aged 43 years

11 George Ashburner Married to Mrs Featherstone both of Barrow
14 a man named Wamsley Killed on the Line near Little Mill run over by the Engine and Train and sadly mutalated his Head and Body
15 Anthony Bamber married to Mary Denney of Lindale at Whitehaven
19 Mr Thos Butler of Dalton married to Miss Robinson only Child of Christopher Robinson Gent Newbarns||

May

12 Died at Barrow Richard James Son of Richard Fisher aged 2 years[66]
9 At St. John's Vicarage Worcester Roger James Esqr formerly of Ulverstone aged 65 years
5 At Broadstone Dalton John Postlethwaite Esqr aged 73 years by his death have lost a good friend
7 very suddenly Elizabeth Wife of Mr John Thompson Cooper Ulverston aged 66 years
15 Died at Ulverstone Mr Samuel Tyson solicitor aged 65 years
In January Mr Thos Fenton of Kendal and late of Spittal Farm Died in Vandiemans Land [Tasmania] aged about 70 years
10 Died in London very suddenly of decease of the Heart John son of Mr Joseph Bragg Cooper Whitehaven and Mariner on board the barque Woodstock recently arrived at London from Jamaica
29 Captn Edward Storey Married to his cousin Isabella Storey bothe of Liverpool

June

9 Died at the residence of J. C. Satterthwait Esqr Milicent Lucinda daughter of the late Robert Michealson Esqr Isle of Barrow.

July

12 Married Mr John Postlethwaite Miller to Tamar Ann youngest daughter of Mr E. Lish Little Mill, near Dalton.
18 Died at Dalton, Thomas Son of James Bolton Ulverston, Where he was out at nurse with Agnes Beatie aged 1 year and 2 months and 3 weeks only one day Ill Inflamation[67]||
25 a robbery commited at Mr Flemings Hotel Barrow by a man who staid a Night there entered Mrs Garnets Room in the morning after she got up, wrenched the locks of two drawers and stole a pocket Book containing Notes and gold to the amount of £50 also a purse containing 20 sovereigns the Telegraph was only finished that morning to transmit the message to Ulverstone He was taken at the Abbey stood his trial at Lanc^{r} on the 7 Augt and sent to be imprisoned in the House of Correction 12 months.

Augt

14 began to shear Wheat led all the wheat 29th and 30th Shore out 8 Sepr
16 son Henry returned from a 3 days visit to Lpool to Barrow Miss Irwin in company He went to Dalton same Evening and to Whitehaven next morning returned to Barrow by Evening Train & returned to Wthaven on the Morning of the 24 inst by Railway at $\frac{1}{4}$ to 6am.
Died at Dalton on the 13 Inst Ann widow of Mr Henry Quail Yeoman aged 86 years

25 Thomas Bowes brought 11 sheep from Fenwick

On Sunday 20 August a young Man Named Sanders was Killed at the foot of Southergate Ulvn by a Horse & Gigg running into him the night being very dark the Horse had taken fright & run away throwing out of the Gigg Mr Stamper & Atkinson Mason

Sept

1 Mrs John Parker with her two daughters & a Cousin Miss Thompson from Kendal paid us a visit by Rail

15 Died at Poulton where he had gone for his Health Mr John Bowes of Liverpool late of Dummara [?] Aged [?]||

Octr

26 Died at Whitehaven Joseph Bragg Cooper aged 74 years

30 Died at Liverpool Alice Wife of Captn John Bleasdale aged 67 years

Novr

Died at Hawcoat Wm Kellet aged 72 years

Decr

5 Died at Liverpool Captn James Storey aged 59 years

10 Died at Barrow Nancy Storey Daughter of Joseph Fisher Butcher aged 6 Months

16 an Inquest was held on the boddy of one of the Men who was covered up by the Brick work falling in at one of the Ore Pits at Roanhead he lived 3 days after being got out, great hopes had been of his recovery

15 Died at Biggar in Walney after a tedious illness, Mary Wife of Mr John Richardson Cragg aged 51 years

24 Died at the Manor House Furness Abbey Frances Widow of the late Mr John Case farmer aged 58 years

22 Henry came to Dalton went to Uston [Ulverston] next day and came to Barrow that night, staid over Sunday W.J. [William James] and his wife and two Drs came next morning Xmas day, Henry returned with them at night & proceeded to Whitehaven next morning 26 Decr

1855

April

6 Good Friday son Henry came from Whitehaven went to Dalton on Saturday & returned at Night went to Dalton on Sunday Afternoon & left there on Monday morning pr train to Wthavn

May

1 Henry took Rheumatic Fever at Wthaven laid up over 6 weeks

Augt

7 Henry came round by Lpool & left Barrow on the 12 to Wthaven||

Jany

14 Died at Dalton Dorothy only Daughter of Mr Thos Towers aged 19 years

14 at Lightburn place Ulverstone Margt relict of the late John Woodburne of Thurston Ville Lancashire Esqr in her 68 th year also same day and place Mary Ann Wife of Thos Woodburn Esqr solicitor in her 28 th year, In Child bed.

18 Died at Newton in Furness Mr Joseph Deason Farmer and Joiner in the 56 year of his age

20 Died at Whitehaven in Middle Church Street, after a long & painful Illness born with Christian meekness & resignation Jane Eldest Daughter of Captn Irwin aged 25 years deeply regretted

Died at Dalton George Ormandy Surgeon aged 53 years

22 Died at Leece John Jackson Mid Town aged 80 years

31 Died at Thurston Ville aged 6 years John Eldest son of Thomas Woodburn Esqr solicitor Lightburn in Ulverstone

Feby

1 Died at Roose Coat Mr Thos Huddlestone Yeoman aged 93

3 A Sailor drowned going to his vessel 11 oclock at night

3 Died at Salthouse Marsh Thos Moss Brickmaker aged 35||

March

1 Died at Barrow Margt Simpson or Fell aged 52 year

2 Died at Rampside Wm Fell labourer aged 74 years father to the above

2 Died at St. Petersburgh Nicholas Emperor of Russia aged 60 It was during the War in the Crimea with Turkey France and England

28 Margaret Fisher[68] Liverpool came to see us she was on a Visit to Miss Letham of Ulverston who had been taken very Ill

April

1 The Children of Barrow & the school Catechized in the Chapel by Revd Thomas Horsfall being the first time of saying

4 Died at Dalton Isabella Wife of Mr Thos. Butler junr., Wine merchant, And only Child of Mr Christopher Robinson Yeoman of Newbarns aged 29 years, much and deservedly respected.

9 Finished corn sowing

Died at Sandscale March 31st Mr Thos Deason Farmer aged 61 years

May

2 Died at the Punch Bowl Inn Crosthwaite near Kendal Mr John Casson Dancing Master of Hawthwaite Bank Broughton in Furness aged 52 years He left a Widow and Nine children. She only confined a few day of her 12th Child.

12 Died Barrow School Mr Antys [Auty?] Child aged 9 months

18 Died at Scales John Hodgson Farm servant aged 24 years||
18 Died at Barrow Mary Jane Daughter of William Barrow aged 1 year
24 Died at Barrow Philip Hartley son of Joseph Fisher Butcher aged 9 years

June

7 Died in Queen Street Ulverston Mr William Richey aged 64 years
11 Died at Salthouse near Barrow Mr James Kellet Yeoman aged 76 years
Died at Barrow on the 7 inst Ellen Wife of Mr John Santer Gas[69] fitter aged 29 years
20 Died at Hawcote Mr Thomas Gibson Yeoman aged 63 years at St John the Baptist Liverpool on the 13 inst Edward Storey, Master Mariner, married to Elizabeth, youngest Daughter of the late Mr Wm Gaskell dyer Ulverston.
Married on the 14 inst at St. Saviours Jersey, by the very Reverend the Dean, the Revd James Taylor, Curate of Dalton-in-Furness, Eldest son of Major General Taylor, of Cheltenham, to Frances Helen, second daughter of Captn Davis of Beauvoir, Jersey.
24 Married at Dalton Mr James Hoggarth Engine Driver to Miss M. A. Hartley both of Barrow
25 Mrs Parker Senr with three children came to see us
29 Died at Barrow James son of Robt Charnley Master Mariner aged 3mths.||

July

1 Mr John Parker his wife Daughter Margt Ann & son Braithwaite with my son Wm J & his son William took dinner and tea with us
5 Daughter Margaret Denney came to see us after an absence of 10 or 11 weeks
8 Son Richard went by train to see Henry at Whitehaven found him better
14 Son Richard with his Drs Margt & Eliza and son Wm went to Fenwick to Thos Bowes Clipping returned on the 15th Do
18 Our Niece Elizabeth Fisher from Liverpool on a visit to Miss Leatham Ulvn came to see us had not been here for 21 years.
23 Died at Barrow Isle Thomas Y. P. Michaelson Esqr. Aged 41 years He was Intered at Walney.
27 Died at Salthouse Marsh Mr Wm Kellet Grocer Aged 49 years

Augt

21 Married at Broughton in Furness by the Revd G. Park M.A. Vicar of Hawkshead, the Revd Thomas Horsfall, Incumbent of Barrow in Furness, Eldest son of the Revd. Thomas Horsfall, of Ripon, Yorkshire to Mary Anne Eldest Daughter of L. P. Myers Esq., Solicitor, Broughton-in-Furness.
22 begun to Shear Shore out on the 8th Septr
29 Miss Mary Bell from Kendal and her cousin Thos Barrow Ulverston drank tea with us her hair had turned quite white aged 42
26 Died in Southergate Elizabeth Widow of Mr Samuel Tyson solicitor Ulverstone aged 56 years||

Sept

11 Died in Barrow Mr Geo. Huddlestone after a long & tedious Illness which he bore with Christian fortitude aged 37 years

Octr

2 Married at Dalton W. Parker Simpson to Miss M Waite both of Rampside
Died at Harrogate, on the 29th September after a few hours Illness, the Revd John Baldwin A.M. of Dalton, late fellow of Christ College Cambridge aged 53 years
Died at Barrow on the 30 September Margaret, relict of late Mr John Gawith Shoemaker of Ulverston aged 79 years
15 Died at Ulverstone Elizabeth wife of Captn James Barrow, late of Barrow in Furness aged 72 years
28 Sunday the Newbarns Chapel closed from duty[70]

Novr

5 Married at Dalton Mr William Case of Manor Farm to Miss Boulton of Park House
6 Died very Suddenly at Lightburn House John Brogden Esq.[71] in the 32 year of his age much and deservedly respected.
7 The Wife of a Labourer named Fowler Killed on the Railway near Paddock Hall she was walking home to Barrow||
6 2 men working in Lindal Railway Tunnel[72] when a blast exploded Killed one and sadly injured the other so that his life was despaired of
7 Married at Trinity Church Whitehaven, by the Revd T. Dalton, B.D. incumbent Mr John Clegg of Rampside to Barbara, third daughter of Mr George Colton of Dendron Yeoman.
11 Died at North Scales, Margaret Simpson aged 81 years formerly of Barrow
22 Mr Wm Turner with his grandson Robt. visited us and with Mr Storey Measured the Waste and Sand in portions to William Fisher John Paxton & Joseph Rawlinson and others

1856

January

16 Died at Burlington House, Hants, the Revd David Cockerton aged 67 years formerly of Emanuel College Cambridge deceased was a native of Dalton-in-Furness.

March

1 James Kendal of Salthouse commited Suicide by hanging himself in his own Granary aged 42
4 Died at Kendal Mary Widow of the late John Bell Kendal and Daughter of the late James Harrison, many years Inn Keeper at Barrow aged 74 years she was deservedly respected||
12 Died in Hart Street Ulverston, Elizabeth the beloved Wife of Mr Edward Storey Master Mariner aged 21 years
24 Begun to sow Oats had done 26th I never saw the land work so well before Sharp dry weather

April

12 Brother Richd & his Daughter Margt. paid us a visit from Ulvn where he staid 3 weeks for his Health, visited Uncle & Aunt on the 19th

May

10 son Henry returned to Whitehaven after a 6 weeks visit at Barrow in Rheumatic fever and had been laid up 6 weeks previous at Whitehaven
Died at Penny Bridge on the 7 inst at the House of Mr Wm Shuttleworth Shoe Maker Miss Betty Dixon, formerly of the low Smithy aged 74
Died at Barrow on the 30th April William son of Mr Henry Bond Master Mariner aged 1 year
Died at Brownsville Pennsylvania on the 15th March Brother William Cock[73] a Native of Stricklandgate Kendal Aged 79 years
Died at Barrow on the 6th May Jane Wife of Mr Henry Bond, Master Mariner aged 43 years
(1866 Husband to the above died of colera very suddenly)||[74]
15 Died in Market Street Ulvn Henry Son of the late Mr John Casson, dancing Master aged 5 years and 9 months.
19 Died at Leece, Mary Widow of the late Mr. Moses Harrison formerly Miller, of Torver, aged 81 years
17 Married at St. Paul's Church, St. Pauls Square, Liverpool, by the Revd. Mr Stafford, Mr Joseph Wright, late of Ulverstone, Emma, second Daughter of William Forshaw Esq., of Liverpool.
31 Died at Carlisle, on the 25 Inst after a lingering Illness born with Christian fortitude and resignation, Mr David Berry Anty [? Auty], aged 26 years, late Master of the Barrow School much respected.

June

13 Died at Barrow Agnes, daughter of Thos King junr aged 4 years
Died at Brownsville Pennsylvania, Anna,[75] relict of Wm. Cock June 7 1856 Aged 75 years

July

7 Died, at Dalton Margaret,[76] Wife of Matthew Denney, and Daughter of William Fisher Barrow Aged 47 years.

January 1882

11 Died at Dalton Matthew Denney husband to the above aged 78 years

Aug

13 Begun to Shear Shore out 6 Septr||
12 Married Mr John Cowx draper Whitehaven, to Mary Ann second daughter of Mr Robt. Case spirit Merchant Ulv.
30 Married Mr Jos Brockbank to Miss Jane Ashburner both of Barrow

Septr

7 Son Henry came to see us Came again on the 27 Septr 1856
18 Died at Leece Mr John Bryer Yeoman aged 71 years
29 Died at Kirkland, Kendal Mary widow of the late Robert Robinson Weaver formerly of Dalton-in-Furness aged 82 years.

Octr

4 Died at Ulverstone, Agnes, relict of the late Robt. Nicholson & Daughter of the late Richard Fisher, Barrow aged 73 years
12 Died at her late residence Bridgeport United States, Rachel Widow of the late John Cock formerly of Kendal, in the 82nd year of her age a member of the Society of Friends.

Novr

3 Died at the Ship Inn Barrow Mr Adam Fleming after a lingering Illness born with patience & fortitude aged 44 years

Decr

16 John Fisher returned from California & America after an absence of Twelve years and four months||[77]

1857

February

15 Died at Barrow Jane Widow of William Shaw Farmer formerly of Dalton aged 88 years
12 Died at Liscard in Cheshire, Mary Daughter of John Richardson Cragg she was inter'd at Whalney Chapel
22 Son Henry with his partner Mr Coulthard paid us a visit for the day also Son W. Jas from Dalton all returned to Dalton for the Night.

March

8 Died at Ulverstone Jane Widow of James Coward Draper Aged 59 years
9 Died At his residence little Urswick Francis Town Esqr aged 59.

April

2 Son John C Fisher left Barrow for Liverpool to sail on the 8th on the steamer City of Washington, (the same Vessel in which he came) for New York her burden 2380 tons.
15 begun to sow Oats had finished on the 20 we wear thrown back on account of the weather so rainey

Died at South Shore on the 4 April the Revd Thos Bryer a Native of Leece formerly incumbent of Marton, and head Master of the Marton Grammar School aged 69 years.||

12 Died at Ulverston Eleanor Daughter of Mr. Edward Storey Master of Victoria Aged 13 months.

28 William Ross Married to Annie Kendal Salthouse

29 Died Suddenly at Leece Elizabeth, Wife of William Duke Grocer much and deservedly regreted Aged 67 years

June

1 Whitmonday Married Isaac Hodgson to Betty Creary both of Barrow

29 married Mr William Mowat Surgeon Dalton, to Eliza, third Daughter of the late Andrew Aspden Esqr, Worsted Spinner, Todmorden.

July

5 Son Henry came from Whitehaven to see his Father who was poorly[78]

Died at Henipen Illinois U.S. June 11th Mary Alice, daughter of Henry Casson late of Holme Nr Burton in Kendal Aged 10 years 5 months and twenty Nine days

31 James Bolton with his family Sailed from Roa for Ireland where He had taken a Farm.

Augt

5 Died at the Hemp Garth Villa Barrow Edward Owen Lath river[79] aged 55 years||

13 Married at Dalton Revd Edward Lesh Curate of Myton Boro' Bridge, Yorkshire, to Miss Sarah Sharp of Ireleth

Died at Collingwood Melbourn Australia on the 20th of May last Mr John Lesh son of Mr Edward Lesh late of Newbarns aged 34 years Married at Melbourne Australia Geo. Case Lesh, late of Newbarns to Elizabeth Dr of Mr Robt Mills of Delgany Co. Wicklow, Ireland.

26 Ralph. Wright. Bolton Sailed from Liverpool for Philadelphia in the Ship Kangeroo, Captn Jefferies.

Septr

2 Son Henry came to Barrow left for Wthaven on the 8th

Octr

7 Richd Fletcher married at Dalton to Sarah Daughter of Mr Joseph Fisher Isle of Barrow.

Novr

16 Died at Overton near Lancaster James Cornelius Saterthwaite, Esqr., of Castle Park, Lancaster, aged 61 years

25 Died in Benson St. Ulverston Miss E. Letham aged 73

Died on 20 Novr Mrs Jane Turner of Liverpool.

Decr

14 Cousin Margt from Liverpool visited us she was superintending the affairs of the late Miss Leathom in Ulverston||
25 Son Henry came to Barrow, returned to Whitehaven on the evening of 27th
24 Died at Tranmere Cheshire Hannah the beloved Wife of Mr Thomas Wright aged 71 years
Married on the 15th Decr Mr T. G. Bisset of Barrow to Miss Julia Myers of Broughton in Furness
25 Died at the Isle of Barrow Mr John Ormandy formerly of Pit Farm Cartmel Aged 71 years

1858

Jany

5 Married Mr Coulthard of the firm of Fisher & Coulthard King Street Drapers Whitehaven to Miss Irwin Daughter of Captn Irwin the Reaper of that port.
4 William Andrew Thompson Barrow Married to Mary Huddleston of U'ston she was sent to Lancaster Castle on the 7th Inst for stealing a Sovereign from a Box at Bradylls Arms [Ulverston]
8 Revd T. Horsfall administered Sacrament at our House to William Fisher aged 82yrs 6mths Mrs Elizabeth Fell 82years on the 21inst. It was (my) wife Margaret Fishers 74th birthday||
20 Married at Dalton James Harwood to Mary Huddleston Widow both of Barrow

March

3 Died on James Terrace Barrow Mr Geo Ashburner son of Geo B. Ashburner Esqr., Elescales, Near Dalton, aged 32 years same day at Parkhouse, Mary Ann Cousin to the above and Daughter of Mr John Case late of Newbiggin aged 12 years
26 Died at Barrow Thos King Junr. aged 31 years
27 Died at Barrow Thos Ashburner sawyer aged 75 years

June

15 Died at Ulverston, Mary the beloved Wife of Mr Peter Butler of the Gill aged 62 years.
15 Married at St. Nicholas Church, by the Revd F. W. Wicks, incumbent Mr Henry Fisher,[80] of the firm Fisher and Coulthard Drapers King Street, Whitehaven to Miss Mary Meals Church Street. On the 19 inst died in Southergate Mr Roger Hesketh Barton, Surgeon aged [?]
on her homeward voyage from Australia, on the 17th May last, Mary wife of Mr Richard Parker, formerly of Ulverston and Daughter of Mrs Bell Dalton gate aged 36 years.
24 Miss Banks from Liverpool visited us in company of Mrs Wm Wright and two Miss Butlers Nieces to Mrs Wright on their way to Rampside||

July

24 Died at Barrow John Hartley grocer Aged 58 years

1859

March

25 Died at Barrow Isle Mr Joseph Fisher farmer Aged 82 years

26 Died at Leece Betty Widow of the late Mr John Jackson farmer aged 84

29 Died at Southergate Ulverston, Captn James Barrow late of Barrow, widely known and greatly respected his remains were intered at Dalton April 2nd aged 85 years.

Died on the 19th March, the Infant twin Dr of Mr Rd. Fletcher Lindal.

Died at Apple Grove Workington, on the 24th March Mr William Bragg Aged 77 years.

Novr

2 Married at Dalton Mr Walton Draper Barrow to Dorothy Eldest Daughter of Mr James Tyson of the Manor Farm.

22 Died suddenly in Market Place Ulverstone Miss Agnes Clark in her 86th year greatly respected by a large circle of friends.

21 Mrs Ramsden[82] gave birth to a son at Abbots House

The Iron Furnaces was opened at Hindpool Barrow Witnessed by several gentlemen who came by special Train on the 18th October owners Messrs Hannah [Hannay] and Schneider, It was a Galla and beautiful day for the season||[83]

21 Married at the Congregational Chapel,[84] Barrow by the Revd James Hamer Mr Wm Ormandy joiner to Miss Frances Casson Daughter of the late John Casson Dancing Master. This being the first Marriage at the above place of Worship the Minister and Sunday School teachers United in presenting the newly Married pair with a handsome family Bible.

Footnotes to Text of Diary

1. Mary Fisher, the second daughter of William and Margaret Fisher.
2. William Fisher's brother, Richard. He was a Lancaster merchant.
3. Manor Farm, near Furness Abbey.
4. Thomas Bowes farmed a fell farm at Fenwick some $2\frac{1}{2}$ miles N.W. of Broughton-in-Furness.
5. Swinside, a fell farm $\frac{1}{2}$ mile south of Fenwick.
6. Dr. William Close, surgeon, apothecary, historian and musician. He introduced vaccination into Furness in 1799, edited the second edition of Thomas West's *Antiquities of Furness* in 1805 and patented a polyphonic trumpet in 1812.
7. One of Fisher's horses.
8. William James, Fisher's second son.
9. At this time, Fisher attended Dalton Church.
10. Parson and White's Directory, 1829, lists John Dixon of Penny Bridge, spade and shovel manufacturer.
11. Fisher's brother-in-law, Henry Cook was a coal merchant and coke burner living at Holme near Burton-in-Kendal.
12. Until 1808 Mary Falshaw kept a school in a calf shed not far from the Fisher farmhouse.
13. Christopher Wilkinson was employed as a weigher of iron ore.
14. Robert Chadburn Gelderd farmed at Redman Hall, Little Urswick.
15. The Quarter Sessions. William Fisher was one of the representatives of the Township of Dalton.
16. This entry is particularly interesting. The Custom House at 'Pile [of] Fouldrey' was situated at Rampside. Sometime between 1752 and 1754 a petition was submitted to the commissioners of His Majesty's Customs arguing for a Custom House at Ulverston; this seems to have been successful and the Custom House was opened in 1766. It has been assumed that when the Ulverston office opened, the Rampside office ceased to function, but Fisher's entry throws some doubt on this.
    See Barnes, F., and Hobbs, J. L., 'John Robinson's Book of Precedents, Part I: Two Ulverston Petitions' Trans. Cumberland and Westmorland Antiquarian and Archaeological Society, Vol. 59 New Series, p. 143.
17. Fisher's horses.
18. William Fisher's sister-in-law.
19. Presumably a 'timber raising' when the roof of a new house was put in place with the help of neighbours.
20. Robert Town was a manufacturer of gingham, check and linen cloth.
21. Black Combe (1969 feet) is some 13 miles north-north-west of Barrow. Traditionally this mountain has been used to forecast good and bad weather in the Low Furness area.
22. John Bolton was the son of an Ulverston apothecary. Born in the town in 1756, he later became a wealthy merchant and ship owner residing at Storrs Hall on the shores of Windermere and in his house in Duke Street, Liverpool. He died in 1837.
23. Such esoteric information is rare in Fisher's diary. It is highly likely that he has copied these facts from a newspaper or tract.
24. It is not clear from this entry whether or not James Picthall taught in Barrow or Ulverston.
25. Jacob Parker held the position of Coast Officer and Coast Waiter.
26. Thomas Dilworth was a quarry proprietor resident at the hamlet of Cocken near Barrow.
27. It seems strange that Fisher should record in December an incident which occurred in January. The burial of the boy is not recorded in the transcript of the Urswick Parish Register for January 1830 or 1831.
28. Parson and White's Directory, 1829, lists two Thomas Boltons, one at Rampside the other at Newton.
29. Pyroligneous acid, derived from wood, was manufactured at Backbarrow.
30. See Fisher's entry for 18th April 1831.
31. See introductory note 19.
32. Little Mill Stile is one mile south of Dalton.
33. Thomas Hodgson was Principal Coast Officer and Coast Waiter at Barrow. This entry is significant for it clearly indicates the presence in the community of Roman Catholics.
34. This could be either Moat Scar near Aldingham or Mort Bank in Morecambe Bay.
35. See Fisher's entry for 24th September 1843.
36. A long-standing custom in Furness. On taking the tenancy of a new farm, the farmer would invite his neighbours to bring their plough teams and help him plough his land. In return he provided food and liquid refreshment. According to William Fleming of Pennington, such an arrangement had 'more

attraction and inducement than the most extravagant wages' (15.4.1815). Certainly the inducements offered by Robert Patterson seem to have ensured a successful boon ploughing if the number of ploughs is taken as a criterion.

37. Matthew Dixon was employed as an iron ore loader.
38. T. Y. P. Michaelson was a member of a Cartmel land-owning family. Soon after 1700 the family acquired by marriage Old Barrow Island between the mainland and Walney Island. Today this island is largely occupied by British Shipbuilders Ltd.
39. Henry William Schneider was one of the great figures in the industrialisation of the Furness area. He and his brother John became interested in the local iron industry in 1839 when they began a thorough geological exploration of the haematite deposits. Later they purchased the Whitriggs mine near Lindal and built Barrow's fourth pier in 1842. In 1851 he discovered the rich Park iron deposit near the present village of Askam and in 1859 he and his partner, Robert Hannay, opened the first iron furnace at Hindpool near Barrow (Fisher's entry for Nov. 21 1859); see *H. W. Schneider of Barrow and Bowness*, by A. G. Banks, 1984.
40. See entry for 21 April 1837 and 11 May 1837.
41. This seems to be a fair copy of an original made on a single sheet of paper within the diary. From the first entry, it seems that the 'Fanny' was carrying slate.
42. The new chapel was built on land given to the community by T. Y. P. Michaelson. See note 38 above.
43. John revisited Barrow on at least two occasions, in 1856 and 1869.
44. Richard Fisher was William's eldest son.
45. William's brother-in-law?
46. This is William Fisher's first mention of the Furness Railway.
47. Thomas Bowes Junior? See entry for 17th January 1844.
48. Probably the most momentous event in the history of Barrow. William Fisher can hardly have appreciated the significance when he recorded these lines.
49. In this rather impersonal way, William Fisher records the death of his granddaughter Elizabeth.
50. Another significant landmark in the industrialisation of the Furness area for the opening of the Rampside-Piel [i.e. Roa Island] line allowed a regular steamer service to be operated between Piel Pier and Fleetwood. See *Early Railway History in Furness* by J. Melville and J. L. Hobbs, Cumberland and Westmorland Antiquarian and Archaeological Society, Tract Series, No. XIII, 1951, p.29.
51. William's brother-in-law?
52. Betty Simpson was the widow of James Simpson, a labourer, and neighbour of the Fishers.
53. William Fisher does not record a subsequent murder trial.
54. James Tyson kept the Burlington Inn.
55. This was the accepted custom for suicides.
56. The first reference to shipbuilding in Barrow. The slipway was part of the ship building and repair works of William Ashburner who built the first Barrow ship. See entry for 15th September 1852.
57. Cumberland and Westmorland wrestling was a popular sport in the nineteenth century. This particular bout, for a prize of £300, attracted over 10,000 spectators, coming from as far away as London, Liverpool and Manchester.
58. The 'Jane Roper' was the first ship launched at Barrow. She was built by William Ashburner and registered as a Schooner of 94 tons.
59. Mary Bolton was William Fisher's second daughter. She was buried at Holy Trinity Church, Ulverston.
60. This storm severely damaged the embankment connecting Roa Island to the mainland and breached Walney Island.
61. By 1852 it was possible to travel by train from Carlisle to Barrow and Piel [Roa Island].
62. James Ramsden, arguably the most important figure in the history of Barrow, came to the Furness area in 1846 as a young man of 23. He became secretary and General Manager of the Furness Railway Company and, later, one of its directors. The archetypal Victorian self-made entrepreneur, he had a vision of a town of 100,000 people, financed by money from the Devonshire and Buccleuch families; he persuaded industrialists to underwrite the docks, shipbuilding, steelworks and the manufacture of jute. He advocated the incorporation of the town and became its first mayor. He was knighted in 1872.
63. The railway line between Barrow and Ulverston was not opened until 1854.
64. The Furness Abbey Hotel was built by the Furness Railway Company in 1847.
65. The congregation used St. George's School, built in 1849 on land provided by the Furness Railway Company. In 1852 the Bishop of Chester granted a licence for the performance of church services in the school. St. George's Church was consecrated in 1861.

66. William Fisher's grandson.
67. Another grandson. Thomas's mother had died in December 1852. See entry for 12th December 1852.
68. Fisher's cousin.
69. In 1854 the Furness Railway Company built a gas works in the Railway Yard to light the Company's premises.
70. See entry of 4th February 1844.
71. John Brogden, Junior, was a member of a family deeply involved in the industrial development of Low Furness and in particular in the construction of the Ulverston to Lancaster Railway, 1853–1857.
72. The tunnel was being widened. See Melville, J., and Hobbs, J. L., *op cit.*
73. William Fisher's brother-in-law.
74. This footnote, dated 1866, seems to refer to Henry Bond.
75. Anna Cock, William's sister-in-law, survived her husband by a mere $7\frac{1}{2}$ weeks.
76. Fisher's eldest daughter. The death of her husband, Matthew, in 1882 has been added to the manuscript.
77. John Fisher was William's third son. He had emigrated to America in 1844. He returned in 1857 (see entry for 2nd April 1857) but visited Barrow again in 1869 by which time both his parents were dead.
78. William Fisher was now 82 years old; this is the first indication in the diary of any illness.
79. Rive is a dialect word meaning to split.
80. William Fisher's youngest son.
81. See introductory note 38.
82. See note 62 above.
83. Furness haematite iron ore was admirably suited to the new Bessemer method of converting iron into steel. Within sixteen years the Barrow Haematite Iron and Steel Company, merely one mile from the Fisher farmhouse had become the largest ironworks and Bessemer plant in the world.
84. The Congregational Chapel had been built in Hindpool Road in 1857.

Personal Names Index